Sounds of War

Aesthetics, Emotions and Chechnya

SUSANNA HAST

E-INTERNATIONAL RELATIONS PUBLISHING

E-International Relations
www.E-IR.info
Bristol, England
2018

ISBN 978-1-910814-35-2 (paperback)
ISBN 978-1-910814-36-9 (e-book)

Production: Michael Tang
Copy-editing: Cameran Clayton
Cover Image: (1) Julia Järvelä and (2) iulia_shev via Depositphotos

A catalogue record for this book is available from the British Library.

E-IR Open Access

Series Editor: Stephen McGlinchey
Editorial Assistance: Majer Ma, Ibitoye Olukosi, Hayden Paulsen, Gaia Rizzi and Andrei Sterescu

E-IR Open Access is a series of scholarly books presented in a format that preferences brevity and accessibility while retaining academic conventions. Each book is available in print and e-book, and is published under a Creative Commons license. As E-International Relations is committed to open access in the fullest sense, free electronic versions of all of our books, including this one, are available on the E-International Relations website.

Find out more at: http://www.e-ir.info/publications

About E-International Relations

E-International Relations is the world's leading open access website for students and scholars of international politics, reaching over three million readers per year. E-IR's daily publications feature expert articles, blogs, reviews and interviews – as well as a range of student learning resources. The website is run by a non-profit organisation based in Bristol, England and staffed by an all-volunteer team of students and scholars.

http://www.e-ir.info

Abstract

Sounds of War is a book on the aesthetics of war experience in Chechnya. It includes theory on, and stories of, compassion, dance, children's agency and love. It is not simply a book to be read, but to be listened to. The chapters begin with the author's own songs expressing research findings and methodology in musical form.

About the Author

Susanna Hast is Academy of Finland postdoctoral researcher with a project "Bodies in War, Bodies in Dance" (2017–2020) at the Theatre Academy Helsinki, University of the Arts. She does artistic research on emotions, embodiment and war; and teaches dance for immigrant and asylum-seeking women in Finland.

Foreword

After I defended my doctoral thesis in 2012, reality hit hard. I found myself with a PhD but unemployed, professionally without purpose. I began to devalue my life because I could not find employment; I was not worthy of a single job. But I also began wondering what it was that I would really like to work with. *Compassion*, that was it. I decided to challenge my miserable state of life, and I need to thank my friends and my husband for the encouragement during that difficult period. I decided that no matter what, I would become happy. Even without a job, I would see the value of my life. Then the day came when I was still without any career prospects, but I felt happy and at peace with myself. Soon after, I received funding for this project.

For two years I was supported by the Finnish Foundations' Post Doc Pool (Alfred Kordelin Foundation and Svenska Kulturfonden), and worked as a visiting fellow and research associate at the Graduate Institute of International and Development Studies (IHEID) in Geneva, Switzerland. I wish to thank Jussi Hanhimäki and Oliver Jütersonke for the opportunity to be affiliated with IHEID.

After we returned to Finland with my family, I found myself unemployed again, but I kept working on this project without any funding for some 9 months. I want to thank my husband whose support is the reason I could become a researcher, and who continues to stand by me, in the face of all the ups and downs, the financial difficulties, and the stress related to the practices of the neoliberal university.

I received funding again in 2016 through the project *Incorporating Vulnerability: a non-fragmented approach to feminist research on violence* in the Gender Studies program of the University of Helsinki. I thank Elina Penttinen, Julian Honkasalo and Ada Schwank for their cooperation and insights during the project. Elina Penttinen's *Joy and International Relations* (2013) is a book which has influenced me greatly.

In 2016 and 2017, I also worked on the project *I am Here* funded by the Finnish Cultural Foundation, and *InHaLe* funded by the Kone Foundation with two great dance pedagogues, Pia Karaspuro and Sibylla Klein, from whom I have learned that research is a practice. Through these projects, I have had the chance to practice non-linguistic communication and sharing through dance while working with immigrant and asylum-seeking women.

I became a post-doctoral researcher at the Aleksanteri Institute, the Centre of Excellence in Russian Studies, at the University of Helsinki for the year 2017, which enabled me to finish this book. I wish to thank all colleagues at the Institute, and in particular Director Markku Kivinen, whose support has been invaluable.

I thank Timo Rehtonen for his generosity, patience and faith in me. I met Timo through his partner, a dear colleague and friend of mine, Tiina Seppälä. Tiina always believed in me, and she believed that a professional musician would take me on board and help me do music. Timo did indeed, even though I could not separate a major chord from a minor chord. I composed the songs in this book together with him. Lacking funding, we simply recorded acoustic versions with just two guitars. He also invited musicians to play with us: Hannu Mikkola, Jarmo Saitajoki, Sami Enbuska, Jari Karjalainen and Jaakko Niemi. I was also lucky to find Timo Kalevi Forss with whom I performed a duet. I thank all these amazing musicians warmly.

I am grateful for opportunities to perform: at the 12th International ETMU Days Conference in 2015, the Annual Aleksanteri Conference 2016, the HYT 50-year celebration 2017, and at many other events and conferences.

I wish to sincerely thank Sara Motta for reviewing this book with such precision and helping me consider what I might do better in the future. I also want to thank E-International Relations' anonymous reviewers for their comments and the Editor-in-Chief Stephen McGlinchey for his cooperation and patience with the manuscript of *Sounds of War*. I wish to thank my sister, Julia Järvelä for drawing the young Chechen woman who sang the song *Daimohk*, to which I refer in Chapter two.

I want to thank fellow capoeristas at Capoeira Senzala Genève. Training with Mestre Timbalada and his group was where everything started: where I found my courage to move, and research with my body. I want to thank Lisset Tinland, who taught me both singing technique and confidence. In Finland, my singing and guitar teacher Ólafur Torfason has helped me grow as a performer. The song *Fifteen Thousand* would not be what it is without him.

I want to thank the many colleagues who have encouraged me. So many times I have felt insecure and these women, my sisters, have lifted me up in solidarity: Noora Kotilainen, Saara Särmä, Leena Vastapuu, Marjaana Jauhola, Tiina Vaittinen, Laura Junka-Aikio, Sofia Laine, and Anni Kangas. They are all doing ground-breaking research and have inspired me to be even more careful and critical, yet kind.

I want to thank Johanna Vuorelma and Maija Lähteenmäki for the cooperation with the Politiikasta journal. Working with such professionals has been a privilege. I thank Miia Halme-Tuomisaari and Allegra Lab Helsinki for their cooperation which has enabled me to develop in terms of scientific communication.

I am forever indebted to my former supervisor Mika Luoma-aho for his friendship, encouragement and brilliant mind (which has produced terms like *musistance*). I thank Roland Bleiker for the invaluable support, as well as Emma Hutchison. I have relied on their writings as much as on their kind words over the past couple of years. I thank Evren Eken, with whom I have shared so many conversations about neuropolitics. I thank Mantas Kvedaravicius who helped me connect with Chechens in the diaspora, and who has offered me precious advice. I am grateful to Nelly Staderini from Médecins Sans Frontières for continuous support and precious exchange of thoughts. I wish to thank Frank Möller and Kia Lindroos for their guidance regarding the world of politics and art. I sincerely thank Swati Parashar for holding my hand, a gift I will not forget. Thank you to all those many confer-ence panel chairs and speakers who allowed me to take up space with my voice and movement. Thank you Catherine Baker, Shine Choi, Synne Dyvik, Dan Öberg, Linda Åhäll, Thomas Gregory, Julia Welland, Victoria Basham and Chris Rossdale for comments and discussion while working on this project. I want to thank that someone who drew me an image of the earth with human bodies in it, and wrote "bodies in the world" on a post-it note after I sang at the ISA Conference in Atlanta (2016).

My family and friends, you have had to listen to my songs and hear me complain about academia. Thank you for your endless support. My boys, Ernesto and Oliver, who have had to tolerate their mum being absent too many times, thank you.

This book will be shared also on my website www.susannahast.com, and you will find plenty of additional material there, including the songs for download, films and photos. I thank Sami Sojonen for his amazing photography and for advice on filming. The films and other materials are audio, visual and audiovisual narrations of my journey as an artist-researcher. I have filmed as much as I could in order to leave a trace of what I was doing for myself but for others too. Even if this is not a participatory research project with research subjects, in many ways this research is a co-production. I have been influenced by Chechen dance and music, the musicians I have played with, colleagues in dance and science, and the individuals who have given me feedback after performances.

Most importantly, I thank those brave and insightful Chechens I had the privilege of meeting. You opened the door for me to understand Chechen dance, culture, customs, religion, history and the wars. Some of you have taken a personal risk by sharing your thoughts with me. Unfortunately, I cannot mention your names, but I keep you close to my heart.

For the eagles

Contents

The Sounds of War

This book's chapters (with the exception of chapter two) are titled with reference to a song and opened with that song's lyrics. You can listen to all the songs featured in this book, and download the full album, on the companion website:

https://www.susannahast.com/sounds-of-war

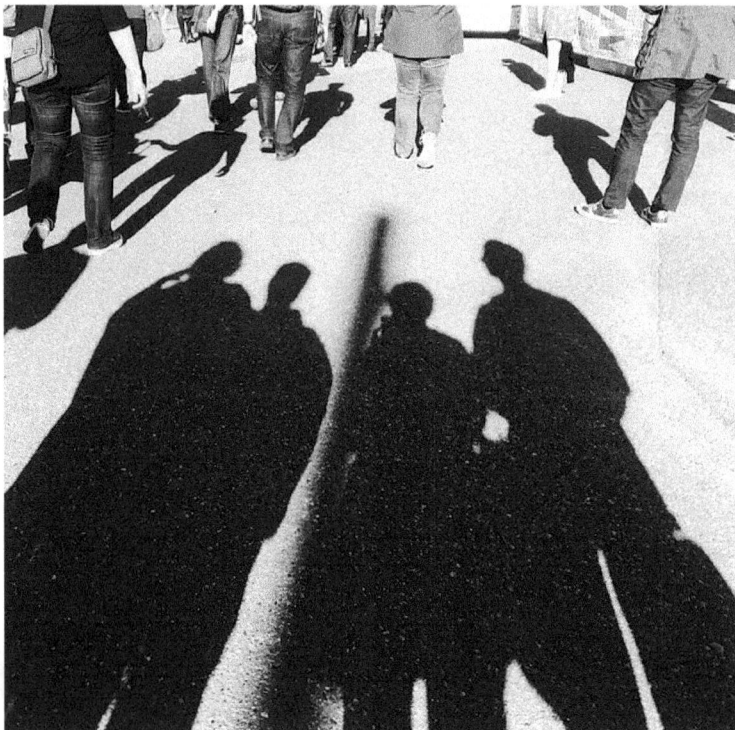

Credits

Lyrics: Susanna Hast
Composing and arrangement: Timo Rehtonen and Susanna Hast

More media resources can be found on Susanna Hast's YouTube page:
https://www.youtube.com/channel/UCr6dZg6WCNHlL3cjEUdv6jQ

1

Deaf

On the field there's a man staring at me
He kneels down, is he hurt, does he bleed?
I don't need, I don't need, to cover my ears

But I feel, I feel the earth, underneath

The life I have
Who could understand
what silence means to a boy like me

On the field the wingless birds
play hide and seek
What I see, is fire sweep where the heartless breathe
I don't need, I don't need, to cover my ears

But I feel, I feel the earth, underneath

The life I have
Who could understand
what silence means to a boy like me

On the field, all alone, the man is gone
In my dream so is fear, haven pure sweet
Hunted down I face the life
and sing to heal

I don't need, I don't need, to cover my ears

The life I have
Who could understand
what silence means to a boy like me

Deaf is about a boy named Sharpuddin. I found Sharpuddin in *A Small Corner of Hell: Dispatches from Chechnya* by Anna Politkovskaya (2003). In September 1999, Sharpuddin, along with hundreds of others, escaped while helicopters circled above. Behind was Grozny, ahead was Ingushetia. Sharpuddin was perhaps six years old. A thin, sad-looking boy, Sharpuddin said that it was nice to be deaf. "The deaf can't hear any of this. And so they're not afraid" (Politkovskaya 2003: 37).

In 1999, Médecins Sans Frontières reported that there was no safe exit for those who wanted to escape Chechnya. There could be no humanitarian aid because of intensive bombardment. The report calls Russia's "fight against terrorism" a collective punishment on the Chechen population (Médecins Sans Frontières 1999). The report states: "The inhabitants of the north who have fled to the south of the republic to escape the bombing of Grozny, Urus Martan, Atchoi Martan, Cernovodsk, and Samachki find themselves on the move again when the villages in the south are attacked by Russian aerial bombings or missiles" (Médecins Sans Frontières 1999).

While I am obsessing about music, sound, hearing, and listening, Sharpuddin is unable to hear. But even if the deaf do not hear, they have an experience of sound. As Oliver Sacks (2000) writes, even the most profoundly deaf can hear various sorts of noises and be sensitive to different vibrations. Maybe Sharpuddin became deaf because of the war, but for him deafness is a blessing in disguise in the war zone. His hearing loss enables him to defy the soundscape of war and thus creates a crack in the affective emotion-scape of fear.

War is also a sonic experience. Sound is central in the war experience of soldiers and civilians (Daughtry 2015). Sound itself can be violent, but sound also organises life in a very fundamental manner. Sharpuddin's war experience was different. He could not be harmed by sound the way those who hear can be, yet being deaf means he is vulnerable in other ways. Sharpuddin's story makes me think: What does war sound like? I will return to this question in Chapter five.[1]

Rationale of the Book

> For a lonely band of human rights activists, Chechnya represents one of the greatest human rights catastrophes of the post-cold war era (Gilligan 2010: 1).

---

[1]   Here is a filmed performance related to the story of Sharpuddin, but also introducing a man called Vakha (ECPR Conference, Glasgow 2014): https://www.youtube.com/watch?v=HHH0OV_2AM8

This book is about emotions and war in Chechnya. War, here, is not investigated through statistics, official reports or the unfolding of events, but through *the aesthetics of non-combatant experience*. In this study, I use autobiographies and films as sources of insight into war and emotions, accompanied by some interview material. The focus is on human capacity, and in particular, human capacity through compassion, dance, children's agency and love. This is not an ethnographic study, but a research project which looks into emotions as they are expressed in art. Emotions are understood as embodied, and instead of a history of emotions in war, this study is an encounter with ideas and insights which easily remain outside the radar in International Relations. Methodological and theoretical discussions occupy much space in this book because of the experimental nature of the work and the elusiveness of human experience.

This introductory chapter, *Deaf*, explores aesthetics as theory/practice/ methodology, and discusses bodily awareness and songwriting as research methods. Chapter two, *Condemned to Hope*, provides the context of the study − the history of war in Chechnya, namely the wars of 1994–1996 and 1999–2009 − and it discusses briefly Chechen culture and the danger of 'othering' when portraying and stilling Chechnya and Chechens.

Chapter three, *Pit*, discusses compassion through the autobiography of doctor Khassan Baiev titled *The Oath: A Surgeon Under Fire,* which he wrote in 2003 after fleeing Chechnya to live in the United States. Baiev treated civilians, Russian soldiers and Chechen rebels alike, alongside female nurses who stayed in Chechnya even after their families left. In this chapter, I explore the concept of compassion at length because the emotion of compassion is the driving force for this study and thus frames the book throughout. Chapter four, *Alia,* continues with compassion, but engages it through visual and auditory means, using the documentary film *Barzakh* and the motion picture *12,* complemented by interview material at the end of the chapter, as sources. The chapter focuses on Chechen dance as a corporeal expression of hope and compassion.

Chapter five, *Fifteen Thousand*, looks at the agency of children through two documentary films: *The Children of Beslan* and *The 3 Rooms of Melancholia*. The chapter argues that children in their daily lives participate in making and shaping political reality. Chapter six *Lonely Night*, returns from film to a narrative source and investigates another autobiography, *Danser sur les Ruines* (2006), written by a young Chechen female journalist Milana Terloeva (real name Bakhaeva) who studied in France as well as in Grozny. Terloeva's story is exceptional in its openness to the role of love in the everyday experience of young people *sur les ruines,* in the ruins.

Memoirs such as Terloeva's and Baiev's can trouble public narratives (see Dyvik 2016) as they express intimate stories of compassion and love in a war zone. The same can be said about the films which visualise the everyday experience and the mundane. The everyday is a space of resistance, not necessarily visible or valuable to an external audience, yet it is in the everyday experience that dominant scripts of war and peace are resisted (see Motta and Seppälä 2016).

The concluding chapter, *Lie*, is divided into two parts. The first part ties together the empirical chapters on compassion, dance, children and love and discusses collective emotions. The second part reflects on the ethics of researching war through aesthetic sensing, proposing that the world can be viewed from new angles with body-based methods and performative politics. At the very end, I introduce the concept of *Musistance* – musical resistance.

The book grows theoretically deeper with each chapter. I begin with the idea of *enactivism* which argues that the mind and body are ontologically one. This concept frames the entire study and is both the starting point of my art-based method and the reason I study emotions through art and the body. I develop enactivism further by using the neuroscientist Antonio Damasio's (2010) work to explore the difference between *emoting* and the *feeling of emotion*. In Chapter three I investigate the bodily basis of compassion, and in Chapter four I continue towards *kinaesthetic empathy*, adopted from dance research. Furthermore, I discuss the role of *synchrony* from research in neuroscience, and present it here in order to show how compassion relates to bodily movement. In Chapter five I explore developmental psychology in order to discuss the emotions of children.

Each chapter begins with a song and a reflection on the songwriting process. The song's purpose is to offer an alternative, auditory experience of the research report. Yet, the chapter is not reducible to the song and neither is the song representative of the chapter – the song and the chapter are in conversation with each other. The musical part of this book is proposed as one possible way to structure and convey the world of embodied, emotional and insightful experience. The lyrics are not composed of ideology or political messages, but thoughts and feelings which emerged during the research process. The songs act as a tool of dialogue between the researcher and the researched. I hope the songs will work as a source of embodied insight into the twilight zone of our creative processes. Rather than offering a new methodology or guidelines, this research attempts to dismantle disembodied ways of producing knowledge. The value of the musical *shape* of research can be evaluated by the reader/listener.

This research is indebted to Feminist Security Studies which opened the path to analysing security and war from the perspective of everyday life (Wibben 2011). I follow the work of Christine Sylvester, who argues that the body is the locus of powerful war experiences (2011: 1). Linda Åhall and Thomas Gregory (2015) point out that the definition of war used in International Relations scholarship is dispassionate and rationalist, resulting in war being viewed as a force-on-force battle. "Emotions are constitutive of war and politics," they state (Åhall and Gregory 2015: xvii). Research on war experience, though crucial in situating war as embodied, has tended to focus on pain and suffering (Dyvik 2016). As Elina Penttinen (2013) writes, in the context of the oppressive and destructive larger structures of war, joy, love and self-healing can seem irrelevant. Yet, war contains all aspects of human life, including creativity. As Leena Vastapuu (2017) writes in her research on young female war veterans in Liberia, hopes and dreams keep individuals afloat through their daily struggles.

This book does not focus on pain and suffering, but on healing and connection. Survivors of violence often rely on self-healing for recovery, especially in war when conventional structures of healing are damaged or destroyed (Mollica 2009). Stories of survival can be central in healing from trauma (Mollica 2009, see also Penttinen 2013). Yet, there is a conflict between a need to offer and receive validation, and a need to forget and the fear of stigmatisation (Lewis Herman 2011). Clarissa Pinkola Estés, in her famous book *Women Who Run with the Wolves* (1996), explores beautifully, through storytelling and folklore, the instinctive powers of women, including intuitive healing and the ability to tend to their own creative fires. This means that human beings are not reducible to their traumas. This book attempts to show this by presenting stories of everyday struggles during war while shedding light on human capacities. I do not mean to say, however, that everyone possesses the capacity for self-healing or resistance. I must emphasise here that it is not my intention to promote strategies of resilience or personal responsibility over the need to address systemic injustices or structures of power. But I am curious about the ways in which people have experienced a meaningful connection with others in spite of, or because of, the suffering caused by war.

When stories are shared, life experiences become validated by the possibility of telling and listening. When shared, stories can be remembered. Stories are a primary way of explaining intentions and actions, producing meaning and making sense of ourselves and others (Wibben 2011). Stories change, they are recreated and their authenticity can be questioned. But it is not the authenticity of stories that interests me, but the aesthetics of stories and the way they make identities which connect and divide people. Stories and memories make people and war alike. Narratives about identity, the state, borders, grievances, *the other,* and so forth enable the willingness to wage war. Narratives about forgiving, healing and surviving construct the self, but also families and communities. Without stories of Chechen war experiences, people would remain statistics and their lives disposable (see Enloe 2014b). We would not know how individuals became empowered and how they changed their lives and their environments. To make lives visible, names known and stories heard is to make life non-disposable. Yet there always remains the risk of re-silencing and abstracting. Even the most inclusive narrations will be exclusive. Most of the stories from Chechnya will never be heard.

The stories we choose to write can become violence, especially if they contribute to what Erin Manning calls *stilling* (2007). Bodies need to be stilled in order to be characterised (2007: xvii). This means that bodies and politics are stabilised in the name of a larger system like the nation-state or the body-politic. The counter-terrorist operation in Chechnya turned male Chechen bodies into potential terrorist bodies which could be abducted, tortured and killed. In Chechen culture, the female body has been stilled through honour (more on honour in Chapter six). Female bodies must live up to the ideals of their communities. Stills are choreographed and composed to set boundaries for people and their imaginations.

To escape the still is to move, and to move out of the frame. I explore in Chapter four how Chechens dancing contradict this stilling and stabilising of bodies. When dancing, the body is active, taking space, communicating emotions. The dancer chooses to be seen. The dancer is not escaping war; not hiding in a cellar; not tortured; not sitting still and quiet as a hostage; not being held in fear, cold and hunger in a pit. The dancer can be suffering, in pain and afraid even, yet, the potential for healing and joy exists in the possibility of self-expression. In Chapter three, I introduce a story of every-day politics that transforms a still in which female bodies are protected by males. A politics of touch emerges in which the corporeal action of women becomes an embodiment of compassion not only in war, but within the framework of a patriarchal society. In Chapter five, children are no longer passive and still representations of fragility, but have their own stories to tell. In Chapter six, the intimate relationships of young women and men are de-stilled from patriarchal structures and a more self-defining agency – a politics of love – is found.

Researching the Aesthetics of War Experience

In researching emotions in war experience, I have chosen to focus on in-depth analysis of a few selected sources. My approach is framed by aesthetics, to which I found my way through the work of Roland Bleiker (see also Ankersmit 1997). Aesthetics is not only the study of art, but everything related to meaning-making. It is not the purpose of an aesthetic analysis to produce descriptions of the world 'as it really is,' but to bring out the insight that art offers through an interaction of sensibilities and thought (Bleiker 2009: 32). Aesthetics redirects thought towards the yet unknown and unimaginable, because it does not rely on conscious thought alone, but thought which is connected to bodily senses and sensations, emotions and the non-conscious.

Whereas mimetic forms of representation attempt to capture the political as realistically as possible,

> An aesthetic approach, by contrast, assumes that there is always a gap between a form of representation and what is represented therewith. Rather than ignoring or seeking to narrow this gap, as mimetic approaches do, aesthetic insight recognises that the inevitable difference between the represented and its representation is the very location of politics (Bleiker 2009: 14).

Bleiker (2017) identifies research on aesthetics as more than research on art – as exploring different ways of writing and sensing. He refers to "opening up thinking space" as the core of aesthetics (262). As part of this process, one can write differently in order to think differently. At the same time, aesthetic analysis needs to be accompanied by self-reflexivity and transparency, because like any perspective, aesthetics also excludes. Choices have to be made. Research practices set the frames which shape the knowledge we produce. In these choices, power is necessarily located and exercised.

In this study, exclusion means, at least, exclusion of systematic ethnographic work. As a mother of two young children, I could not travel for extended periods. Moreover, building trust (both ways) is a long and complicated process especially in the current political climate of fear in Chechnya. This fear affects also the Chechen diaspora. When I finally decided to travel, I was advised against it because it was not safe. In early 2016, President Kadyrov's position was unclear, and journalists had been beaten at the border of Ingushetia. Fortunately, I was able to meet and interview some Chechens in Europe. But I did not want people to have to relive their traumas, so I did not ask difficult questions. I also did not want the children present to hear difficult conversations. I also had to leave out some discussions because the content would risk revealing individual identities.

For the interview material included, I have chosen to use pseudonyms without the location or date of the interviews. These precautions might seem extreme, but during my interview with Ali and Said (2017), it became clear there was a real danger to those who criticised the regime. This might not be in the form of a personal threat, but a threat to the entire family and clan. I asked for permission to publish critical statements after the interviews because interviewees repeatedly voiced their concern when I was taking notes.

Thus, the choice here is an aesthetic analysis of autobiographies and films, with some supplemental interview material added. As Bleiker (2017: 261) advises, "An aesthetic approach to the political has to avoid the hubris associated with the idea that we can advance the kind of grand theories that offer objective and overarching explanations of the world." This research is not meant to be generalized. I do not present one big discovery but rather pieces of a very complex puzzle. This research makes visible new aspects of war and war experience, and situates compassion, love and children's agency at the centre of analysis. I adhere to Bleiker's call for aesthetic engagement to become "political and politically disruptive in the most fundamental way: by challenging the boundaries of what is visible and invisible, thinkable and unthinkable and thus of what can and cannot be debated in politics" (2017: 262).

I view the autobiographies and films analysed in this study as art and art is political (see Lindroos and Möller 2017). As Butler and Bleiker argue, "Art becomes political because it can challenge how we see and conceptualize the world around us" (2017: 112). Art is a sensory experience for the creator and the spectator and a means of political ordering and transformation. The authors of the autobiographies I analyse witnessed war first-hand, and the documentarists captured the aftermath through their camera lenses. Filmmakers sometimes exposed themselves to personal risk entering the (post-)war zone without permission. Such documentary films also relate to debates on the spectatorship of suffering and humanitarianism (see Hesford 2011; Kotilainen 2016). Yet, the films chosen here do not rely on macabre aesthetics – visualisations of violence – but rather the more mundane imagery of human suffering. Because of the lack of violent scenes, the films leave room for perspectives on agency beyond victimhood.

The motion picture *12* I analyse in Chapter four is a "witness of conviction" (Gibbon 2010: 105) and it reflects on how the Chechen wars have been dealt with, or rather not dealt with, in Russia. Such witnesses of conviction, or of "inner knowing," as Jill Gibbon explains (2010: 105), do not have to be eye witnesses. The idea of art as a witness of conviction comes from war art which became popular around 1917, and which derived from the romantic idea of art as the source of authentic values. Here art is not seen as a witness of the authentic, but a witness which can disturb established narratives and bring forward new insights. Sometimes the insights come from an absence, sometimes from a presence. Yet, the absence of visual representation is not necessarily an absence at all (Chowdhury 2016: 42). There can be an auditory presence, or a presence which comes forward by suggesting the unknowability of experiences of violence. For me, researching war is a negotiation between what is knowable, visible, audible and what is not. Somewhere between the sensual experience, curiosity and doubt, insight emerges. Like Bleiker (2009), I prefer the term insight to knowledge, for it is more open-ended and leans more toward the senses. Knowledge is often interpreted as rational and instrumental in ways which exclude intuition and emotion. For me, insight is in the present – it is experiential and lived corporeally.

Autoaesthetics

This study investigates the politics in-between the representation and the represented, and it 'reoccupies the political' (Seppälä 2017) by situating the researcher as a political subject. To reoccupy the political is to perform and create art – to receive and to give. I have documented my artistic journey as much as I could on social media and YouTube. I try to make visible the pain and pleasure of performative politics by refusing to conceal my presence (Daigle 2006). In fact, it turned out to be impossible to 'just write about Chechnya,' because every single day I did research I had to negotiate difference and otherness. I could never escape myself, nor the ethics and aesthetics of othering.

But rather than calling it autobiography, storytelling or narrative politics (Bleiker and Brigg 2010; Daigle 2006; Dauphinée 2007; Inayatullah 2011; Inayatullah and Dauphinée 2016), I use the term *autoaesthetics*. Auto-aesthetics refers to the role of the self in research, but in addition to the autobiographical self, it focuses on the aesthetics of performance and vulnerability. Because this study blurs the boundary between science and art, it allows encounters with a world we do not normally see (Dauphinée 2013). It does not involve simply writing from the inside but producing aesthetic sensations that go beyond writing.

Autoaesthetics is intimate and rigorous artistic scholarship. Theory is not somewhere outside of me. As a researcher, I join with and journey with the research material. I am a political subject who always returns to the intimate. Not only do I write the body and the body's journey in, but I research and express the results corporeally and melodically. To be precise, I had to resort to performance because so much of the body could not be written in this book. Because of these choices, I have also had to reflect on the ethics of my aesthetics. Previously I would contemplate how distanced my academic writing was from the lived experiences of my research subjects. Now I have to consider what my dancing and singing *does* – what feelings, meanings, and ideas my artistic creations potentially produce.

Writing the self in reflexively means acknowledging the relationship between the self and the other. The danger, I have discovered, is the almost paralysing thought that one's research may never be ethical enough. Sara Ahmed (2004c) discusses, in the context of whiteness studies, the declaratory nature of self-reflexivity, in which a declaration of one's shame about being a racist is assumed to make one non-racist. That is, by declaring my guilt over my privilege, I relieve myself of that guilt. Andrea Smith (2013) is concerned that rather than creating political projects to change structures of domination, confessions of privilege become political projects in and of themselves. Emphasising one's privileged position can be counterproductive and may even construct privilege and hierarchy rather than dismantle it. There is a danger in using solidarity and the discourse of privilege as an identity project – ethical reflection may have the effect of making me feel good about myself. Tiina Seppälä (2016) has chosen to write about her privilege, not to confess or declare, but to show how some of her research practices changed when she tried to unlearn privilege. I share that intention.

I decided to continue with an art-based approach even at the risk of producing something unethical, because that same risk is embedded in all forms of expression and all means of exchanging insight and knowledge. I am accountable for any mistakes to Chechens first and foremost.

Art-Based Research

This is a multidisciplinary and artistic study that takes a stand for seeking out insight wherever and however it comes about. When I wrote songs about the wars in Chechnya in the winter of 2014, I did not consider songwriting a research method, nor did I realise that I was following an established practice of art-based or creative research design, such as those developed in the field of Critical Security Studies (Salter and Mutlu 2013). If the main research challenge is a puzzle, it can be addressed with all means available. As Bleiker (2003: 420) writes, "A source may stem from this or that discipline, it may be academically sanctioned or not, expressed in prose or poetic form, it may be language based or visual or musical or take any other shape or form: it is legitimate as long as it helps to illuminate the puzzle in question." Thus, the musical, the narrative and the theoretical will hopefully blend into a meaningful mixture that interests readers inside and outside academia.

Sometimes art-based methods are not viewed as 'real' research (MacKenzie 2008). However, art-based method allows for more creative freedom to engage with both the research topic and society because the researcher can experiment with different forms and shapes, some of which may be more approachable to a wider audience. Art-based research also invites the reader to get closer to the author (see Manovski 2014). Knowles and Cole (2008: 29) describe arts-informed research as "bringing together the systematic and rigorous qualities of conventional qualitative methodologies with the artistic, disciplined and imaginative qualities of the arts." Art connects people, encourages empathy and advances a more respectful and dialogical society. In this project art is present in all aspects, from the research process to the final products. This research project is an example of "thinking in, through and with art" (Borgdorff 2011: 44).

Art-based method, also called artistic research, performative research or practice-as-research, means that art is not extra or secondary, but central. The art-based method encourages speaking with the body and using non-textual communication. Since the study itself examines the body in lived experience, a mere textual representation would be inadequate. In academic writing, 'rational thought' is often privileged in an attempt to contain violence in representations that sustain our immunity and distance from it (Daughtry 2015). Thus, there are ethical and political implications in writing differently (Daigle 2016). This does not mean we should abandon academic writing but, rather, we should take into account that it is not the only means of scholarship available.

For me, this project has been a process of unlearning: in music I can abandon explanations, jargon and objectivity by concentrating instead on the politics of passion and art. This politics of art is meant to reveal human potential, above all. Like Jacques Rancière (2008), I am critical of a cause and effect relation-ship between art and political change, because there is no fixed continuation of sensing from the product of art to the spectator's experience. As Rancière puts it, art's influence is not based on the mediation of messages, offering of role models or warning examples. Art affects through organising bodies, and by defining ways of being together and being separated. Art's influence is, then, not based on ethical immediacy or mediation of representation, but aesthetics. Aesthetic influence ruptures any linear connection between art and audience; that is, there are no predefined sensorimotor consequences in an aesthetic experience. Aesthetic influence is then a conflict in different orders of sensing, and conflict is the essence of the political. The political, for Rancière, is more than a struggle for power, it means action which moulds the sensual settings within which shared properties are defined. A politics of aesthetics gives birth to new capacities and challenges – what is seen as possible. It is not so much the content, but the form of art which makes it political, and this applies to the art I have created.

The shapes and forms of art expand what is seen as possible in scientific inquiry. The songs re-situate bodies and redefine capacities in unpredictable ways. They rupture the tissue of the senses by demanding different perceptions and feelings. I mix and confuse styles, moods and sensory sources on purpose. In the songs, victims of war become more than victims, and the researcher becomes aware of the passions which are deemed inappropriate. Art is not fiction which enters the real world – it is the real world.

Songwriting

Human beings are musical and have a special musical memory. In *Musicophilia,* Oliver Sacks (2008) writes that, with few exceptions, people are able to perceive music and its nuances like melody, rhythm, pitch and harmony. Moreover, musical experience is emotional, visceral, and muscular. Our bodies follow the narrative of a piece often non-consciously. Amazingly, we are able to recreate music in our minds following the original pitch and tempo due to a special musical memory. This musical memory enables Alzheimer's patients to remember music even when they have lost their autobiographical selves (see Sacks 2008).

Assal Habibi and Antonio Damasio (2014) write that music has a profound impact on the human being. Music can alter neural systems, such as those associated with auditory and motor processing, but it also affects the regions of the brain responsible for regulation processes (homeostasis). Music induces feelings which are informative and nourishing at the individual level, but it can also act at the collective level. Habibi and Damasio (2014: 93) hypothesise that "music can engage innate physiological action programs and, by doing so help restore the physiological state to a range of relative homeostatic balance."

The aesthetics of music is a non-fragmented experience. "There is no musician here and instrument there and music somewhere else and audience out there taking it all in" (Merrell 2003: 137). To take this further, when we listen to music we integrate tone, timbre, pitch, melody and rhythm non-consciously so as to experience music (see Sacks 2008). Music permeates the scene and beings in it. When we analyse music intellectually, we can distinguish different components, but when we enjoy music aesthetically, we hear its totality, even if we appreciate certain elements more than others.

Songwriting became my method accidentally. In fact, it was not a conscious but an intuitive choice. Put another way, doing without thinking or planning created the method. The amateurish songwriting is visible in the unconventional structures of many of the songs. Not knowing how to write music was an opportunity to write and compose freely in the beginning. Learning to write music, I discovered a new way of experiencing research. Reading Sacks, I realised how there is nothing peculiar about the attempt to experience the world through melodies. Borrowing Patricia Leavy's (2015) concept, music is a *shape* in the research process. Incorporating music, scholarship emerges in a different form, and the songwriting itself shapes the content and how it is received. Because music is passionate and playful, it has the power to restructure thinking and disrupt established hierarchies. Considering the role music plays in human life, my choice to sing, record and perform becomes political.

Songwriting is poetic writing that goes beyond the textual. Songwriting allows the unspeakable to be said. Non-linguistic elements such as melody, harmony, rhythm, mood, tempo and tone always live in the moment as a corporeal exchange of meanings and feelings (Hast 2016). The words I write are whispers of my body – my bones, skin, nerves, blood, cells and organs. Sound alters my body and consciousness, and hopefully others' too. My words may be interpreted and misinterpreted in any number of ways, and even my own mind changes the meanings depending on the situation or my mood.

The songs here are not representations of Chechnya, or Chechen war experience. They are a body swinging to rhythms and a mind travelling to known or unknown places. I am not the voice of the victims of war. I am not even a messenger. As Cynthia Milton (2017: 132) argues, "art is not bound to truth." Art investigates competing narratives and can thus contradict official histories. The music I created does not attempt to grasp the victim's truth, but it does raise questions about commodification and exploitation (see Lindroos and Möller 2017). Art does not have to be a presentation of something (reality or truth), it is a presentation of itself. This means, according to Lindroos and Möller (2017), that art can have the capacity to be a witness through the very act of its presentation. The songs I have written are an important part of this research, but they also stand alone as 'just music.' There is a curious entanglement of art as witness in this research, witnessing which I have not entirely figured out. Film is a witness, the autobiographies are witness testimonials, and I, myself, am a witness. Witnessing permeates all levels.

The playfulness of music-making is my way of practising "feminist resistance to abstraction" (Wibben 2011: 2). Through the act of composing and songwriting, I resist the dualisms of body/mind and knowledge/emotion. I rely on interoception (sensory signals originating inside of the body), exteroception (observing the outside world) and proprioception or the kinaesthetic sense (movement and relative positions of the parts of the body) to ensure an awareness of the felt sense, the *lived experience* (Merleau-Ponty 1964). That the *lived body* is both conscious and non-conscious is the epistemological foundation of this research. By singing, I hope to reach the felt sense of the listener, and for the listener to become a participant in an exchange of emotions. When performed and heard, the songs negotiate power relations in that they help determine how and what we know. The songs bring pain too: the pain of storytelling and aesthetic pain. Singing about war or scientific findings is not easy. There is awkwardness and vulnerability embedded in the project which I cannot escape – and perhaps, should not escape. I return to this discussion in the conclusion.

Songwriting begins with the body; it makes the body move and the moving body makes the songs. Songwriting is also an emotional endeavour and it can feel like being haunted by something. Sometimes we write from our own dark places even when we write about others (Lamott 1995). Songwriting is necessarily personal but it carries with it the possibility that some aspects of the research subject will become more visible. To quote McNiff (2008: 37),

> Art embraces ordinary things with an eye for their unusual and extraordinary qualities. The artist looks at banal phenomena from a perspective of aesthetic significance and gives them a value that they do not normally have. This way of relating to things may have more social significance than one might at first imagine.

When I was at a loss with the need to domesticate 'knowledge' about war, I found a way out through music. When I was unable to unemotionally intellectualise and analyse someone's war experience, I could express the way I needed to and explicitly with emotion through music. As I composed and wrote the lyrics, I formed a different relationship to my research material and learned different ways of thinking by composing. The search for a chord or a word; the rehearsal and repetition, had a profound impact on my capacity to appreciate the mundane. When I began cooperating with Timo Rehtonen and other musicians, the artistic process took a cooperative turn. My collaborators had no knowledge of my research (or interest, necessarily), but they were making this music with me and were thus part of the research process. I could bring professional musicians into that same dialogue and process of producing embodied sensibility and thought on war, healing and Chechnya. I found new audiences outside the academic context by bringing the music to public events, clubs and a music festival. I have begun calling such performative politics *musistance* – musical resistance, a concept to which I return in the concluding chapter.

What does war sound like? Can it sound like funk music? Khassan Baiev, a Chechen surgeon, whose war experience I discuss in the following chapter, needed something to calm his anxiety as he worked to save people's lives and limbs. Sleep-deprived and exhausted, he used breathing and exercise to calm his nerves. His father had suggested that he listen to music – not slow songs but music with a strong rhythm. Baiev followed his father's advice and played this type of music between operations until one of the nurses com-plained that it was not appropriate because people were suffering. Others might think they were having a good time. Music has a way of inciting emotions, and shame can be one of them. In this case, being perceived as enjoying oneself or having fun amidst war became shameful even though it brought relief.

Embodied Insight

Mark Johnson (2007), who has researched how bodily experience gives rise to reasoning and conceptualisation for some 30 years now, suggests that aesthetics is the key to understanding the visceral origins of meaning. For Johnson (2007: x), aesthetics is broader than the study of art or aesthetic experience, it is "the study of everything that goes into the human capacity to make and experience meaning." As Johnson argues, cognitive neuroscience is offering us proof of how non-conscious thought and feeling are at the core of reasoning and meaning-making. Mind and body as ontologically one means that thought emerges via the recruitment of various sensorimotor capacities. This is why I write about the body of the researcher, and thus try to dismantle disembodied research methods. Such methods disregard the body and see the mind (separate from the rest of the body) as doing the analysing and conceptualising work.

The body of the researcher is an active tool in meaning-making. Insight is then produced *in-between bodies*. The *embodied insight* then does not come from the self alone, but from a sensibility in relation to the other. The body of the researched affects my body; thus, I am not in complete control of that bodily exchange.

The body enables and restricts what and how we observe, know and process. According to Damasio (2010), body mapping, to which I will return later, underpins the self process in conscious minds and the representations of the world external to the organism. The ability to know the outer world depends on the ability to know the inner world. Research is learning, and learning does not take place in a brain independent of (the rest of) the body. Thus, I am looking at learning beyond the dualism of mind and body. Learning is not just the cognitive processing of symbolic information (numbers, words, shapes, etc.) taking place in the brain (Anttila 2013); through the process of sensing and emoting in interaction with others, learning *changes* the body. Our conscious awareness of our bodily processes arises when the body is in pain, sick or experiencing pleasure, but most of the time we can be unaware of our bodies. Likewise, we are often unaware of how the body learns, perceives and communicates. But it is possible to become mindful of the body, to direct attention to bodily experiences and changes in the body's state (Anttila 2013).

Singing is an embodied method – it necessitates the use of voice, breathing technique, volume and bodily exercise. But there are many other ways I have utilised the body while researching. Since this book is about the sounds of war, I have tried to pay attention to different sounds. Listening to a film without watching it is one example. The soundscape without images helps bring focus to the embodied insights coming from senses the researcher might easily ignore, such as hearing. Without visual stimuli it is difficult to ignore the sound of a helicopter flying around, for example. Sounds make one remember, they are sonic somatic markers. Listening is a way to see further. I have tapped and clapped to the rhythms of the films I have analysed. I have danced. I have used mirroring/mimicking, synchronous movement and kinaesthetic empathy as theory and as practice; that is, I have tried to embody that which I have seen. I have not simply watched films, but I have moved with the people in them as part of an embodied methodology.[2] I return to this in Chapter four.

To read and sense with the body is to read and sense with emotion, without separating thinking from emoting. Davies and Spencer (2010) argue for what they call radical empiricism which refuses an epistemological cut between subject and object, and acknowledges that emotion in fieldwork can be used to inform the research. But it is not only fieldwork that needs to rethink the role of emotions in research. The disregarding of emotions in research is associated with the construction of emotions as gendered and feminised – emotionality as a sign of weakness (Parashar 2011). Positions, experiences and emotions make us the readers and interpreters we are. Des Fitzgerald (2013) even sees emotions as having an important role in the neurosciences and psychology – fields which study emotions.

By attending to emotion, I found my way to the root of a research finding. To attend to emotions is to take emotional/intuitive insight seriously. For me it meant battling despair and perception bias when my attention was directed towards the negative, threatening and dangerous. It meant observing physical

---

2   see https://www.youtube.com/channel/UCr6dZg6WCNHlL3cjEUdv6jQ).

changes in order to stop at crucial moments to re-read or re-watch something that moved and affected me but that I struggled to write about. It meant looking into my own lived body as a site of insight. Sometimes I cried, sometimes I laughed, sometimes I noticed my pulse change, or my body shake or twist. Very often I felt anxious or excited. I became a witness to violence and was at times unemotional, and at other times oversensitive. When I analysed a play dealing with the school siege of Beslan (Hast 2017), I left the theatre feeling empty, without having shed a single tear. I realised that the absence of visual and linguistic representations of suffering in the play were in fact a presence of non-discursive emoting. From concerns over my own emotionless state, I became curious about children's emotions and how they might be embodied.

When minding emotions and sensations, the research argument does not always manifest in language but remains lingering inside the skin, on the surface of the skin, on the tip of the tongue, within the cramps of the stomach, with the changes in breathing, with the sweaty armpits and cold fingers. The body's experience is always temporary. There is no return to the moment of sensing once it has passed. Yet, the momentary lived experience is the source of knowledge and insight. Because there might never be a linear link between the sensory input and the argument, it might be necessary to come up with different means to let knowledge flow from body to body more directly and with more vulnerability. Ahmed (2017: 13) writes about sweaty concepts which emerge from a "description of a body that is not at home in the world" and "a bodily experience that is trying." Eliminating the effort and the sweat is an academic aim – we have been trained to tidy our texts from the personal struggle.

Aesthetics is an exercise of the body; it is meaning-making through aware-ness of sensory experience. These meanings are not mimetic representations of reality, but relationships with the world, encounters with the other. The body knows, remembers and feels, and I take emotional/intuitive insight seriously. Emotion brought me to movement, and the impact of Chechen dance on my body helped me to develop the embodied method. Dancing became a way of researching embodiment and this happened because I no longer separated thinking from the body.

Dance is all about the body. It is a non-linguistic yet often narrative form. A dancer can begin to remember herself, and grow to remember something lost (Monni 1995). Muscle memory is a deep automatic memory, but movement itself is a journey of investigation. We can find ways of being through the practise of art. We can – and do – think through the body. Yet often, like Merrell (2003) points out, we view our bodies as 'other' to the self, the self's possession. But we already have the knowing body, the remembering body. The lived body is a site of knowing (Green 2002; Rouhiainen 2008), and movement is at the root of our sense of agency – it generates our sense of time and space (Sheets-Johnstone 2011). As Merleau-Ponty (1964: 5) writes, "The body, in turn, is wholly animated, and all its functions contribute to the perception of objects – an activity long considered by philosophy to be pure knowledge." Yet, this knowing is, to a great extent, automatic and non-conscious. It would be impossible to function if one had to be consciously aware of everything. This goes for research as well. Most bodily sensations are unattended to, yet they influence the way the researcher perceives and makes sense of the external world. So rather than being aware of all kinds of sensations, the embodied method means not writing emotions and sensations out. As a researcher, embodied insight comes from not denying the existence of the living body in the research process.

Body and Mind as One

So far, I have written about the importance of aesthetics and sensing with bodily awareness, but to make embodied insight a research practice, body-mind dualism must be overcome. My thinking about emotions and aesthetics has been greatly influenced by Floyd Merrell's (2003) concept of *bodymind*. Bodymind is body and mind together, as a singularity. Bodymind does before the mind becomes aware. This means that instead of thinking that the body affects the mind, and the mind affects the body, this singularity makes the two inseparable. To quote Damasio (2010: 200):

> [...] the body proper remains inseparably attached to the brain at all times. This attachment underlies the generation of primordial feelings and the unique relationship between the body, as object, and the brain that represents that object. When we make maps of objects and events out in the world, those objects and events remain out in the world. When we map our body's objects and events, they are inside the organism and they do not go anywhere. They act on the brain but can be acted upon at any time, forming a resonating loop that achieves something akin to a body-mind fusion.

The body-mind connection is quite amazing. Take phantom pregnancy, for example: all the possible physical symptoms of a pregnancy, but no baby (see Ramachandran and Blakeslee 1998). The causes and mechanisms of phantom pregnancy are unknown, but the condition means that the mind can cause the body to develop signs of pregnancy. If the mind can do this, what else can it do to the body? Conversely, what can the body do to the mind? Or, what do they do together?

Evan Thompson (2007: ix) suggests that there is a "deep continuity of mind in life." Where there is life, there is mind. This means that mental life is also bodily life and situated in the world. This approach is called *enactivism*, and it was originally coined by Varela, Thompson and Rosch in *The Embodied Mind* (1993). It is characterised by multidisciplinarity, combining neuroscience, phenomenology, biology, psychology – and here the study of politics. Giovanna Colombetti draws on phenomenological philosophies and likewise understands the body though enactivism. Enactivism refers to embodiment: "the mind is enacted or brought forth by the living organism by virtue of its specific organization and its interaction in the world" (Colombetti 2012: xiv). The body here does not mean only the sensorimotor system (which links sensory input to motor action) but a living body which includes the viscera, the circulatory system, the immune system and the endocrine system – these are all related to the functions of the mind. The enactive approach helps to frame the mind and body as ontologically one, and one in the world. Thus, embodied insight is an enacted bodymind.

The above discussion implies that if we abandon the separations between mind and body and emotion and cognition, the nature of emotions like compassion become less clear. Is compassion felt somewhere in the body? Does compassion manifest in certain action tendencies? Can compassion be triggered by sensing the emotions or movements of another body? And how much thinking is involved? To unpack some of these questions, it helps to separate emoting in the body from the conscious feeling of emotion. This does not mean another body-mind separation, but recognising emoting as a process. The separation is then about non-conscious and pre-discursive felt sense, and the conscious processing of the felt sense. I explain this next with the help of Antonio Damasio's (2010) work.

Emotions and Emoting

Emotions emerge interpersonally, circulating between bodies and signs, delineating and binding together bodies and nations (Ahmed 2004a; Ahmed 2004b). What Ahmed means is that emotions do not simply belong to the individual, they are not a property nor do they reside in a person; but they move, in time and space, in a rippling effect. This means emotions are shared collectively, and are integral for understanding war. But how to study emotions in International Relations? Marysia Zalewski (2015: 35) wonders if an affective method is too problematic, and asks: "Unless writing a poem or a novel, can one represent a sense of emotional and affective intensity?" Bleiker and Hutchison (2008b) propose that, indeed, aesthetic insights are particularly suited to capturing emotions, because the emotions of a person cannot be easily known or communicated authentically. Art does not have to represent objects or events as realistically as possible. It can instead communicate emotional relationships. Aesthetic sensing encourages affective methods for it deconstructs the artificial border between objective and subjective sources of embodied insight.

I do not think that the difficulties in studying emotions (with emotion) in International Relations is a problem of representation but a problem born out of the dualism of emotion and cognition. The dualism of emotion and cognition is easily overcome, for example, by looking into neuroscience. In fact, studies of emotion in the field of political science cannot escape the psychological and neurological nature of emoting. Affects and emotions call for a multidisciplinary approach (Saeidi and Turcotte 2011; Crawford 2014; Jeffery 2014). The argument is this: There is no separation between cognition and emotion; cognition is always already affective (Colombetti 2012). As Damasio (2010) argues, there is not even consciousness without feeling. According to Damasio, the self with a body, mind and past are known to the mind because they generate emotions and feeling. Feelings accomplish the separation between the self and that which is not the self. He calls these somatic markers emotion-based signals. We would not know who we are unless we had a constant emotional bond to the internal and external world. For William Connolly (2002), somatic markers make it possible to perceive and decide in a timely manner. Thus, we would not know what to do without somatic markers.

Damasio has studied patients with brain damage affecting their ability to make decisions. Because the patients could not associate emotions with their decision-making process, they engaged in endless cost-benefit calculations (Damasio 2009). Emotions are necessary for timely decision-making, but decision making is also partly non-conscious. Damasio (2010) and Jonathan Haidt (2000) acknowledge the importance of gut feeling, or intuition, in decision-making. A research on emotions then needs to acknowledge not only how important emotions are for decision-making in the lived experience of the research subject, but also how researching, itself, relies on emotions, and there is no escape from them.

Affect and emotion are commonly separated with affect being the non-conscious corporeal experience while emotion is conscious, anchored in language and meaning (Hoggett and Thompson 2012; Manning 2007). Colombetti (2014), who also separates affect from emotion, recognises that Damasio's conception of emotion is broader than is typically assumed in affective science because it affirms that basic life-sustaining processes are continuous with mental processes. The reason I like to refer to emotion rather than affect, is that I take emotion as embodied all the way through both the conscious and the non-conscious.

Damasio (2010) separates the physical, non-conscious bodily process that is emotion from the *feeling of emotion*, which happens when the individual becomes aware. Emotions are automated programs of actions carried out by our bodies and manifested in facial expressions, postures and visceral changes. Feelings of emotions, instead, are "*perceptions* of what happens in our body and mind when we are emoting" (Damasio, 2010: 109, emphasis in original). What follows emoting are brain maps entering consciousness as images (visual and non-visual), that are perceiving what is going on in the body.

In using conceptions of emotion and emoting I want to emphasise corporeality in awareness and beyond it. In order to avoid the Cartesian body/mind distinction I will not try to draw a strict line between emotion and the feeling of emotion. I believe this is the essence of Damasio's conceptualisation as well. The body speaks, the body knows, and the mind is enacted through the body. There is a deep continuity from mind to body and from body to mind, from emoting to the feeling of emotion and from the feeling of emotion to emoting. It is the bodymind as singularity.

Then how about the relationship between perception and emotion? Emotion affects the way we perceive, what we perceive, how we interpret what we perceive, what perceptions we store in our memories, and what we bring forth from our memories when need be. Emotions affect our brain and bodily processes, like cognitive processes such as memory and attention (see Damasio 2010). Emotions themselves are triggered by objects or events happening in the moment, or which have happened in the past and are being recalled. Images of what is happening or has happened, or what one imagines, are processed as images in different regions of the brain.

Damasio (2010) explains that we perceive by engagement, not passive reception. Maps of objects *in movement* are assembled in the brain. The feeling of emotion is based on a special relationship between the brain and the body: the capacity to map one's own bodily processes as well as those of others. According to Damasio, emotions are communicated through the highly trained observation of postures and faces. He states that, "feeling attribution has nothing to do with language" (2010: 167). This is something to chew for a political scientist, but Damasio refers namely to person-to-person encounters of intersubjectivity in which the individual reads the body's cues to learn about the emotional state of the other person.

As already stated, emotions are not wholly private experiences, but are transmitted between individuals, even groups (see the concluding chapter for more on collective emotions). This is a social and biological process. Teresa Brennan (2004) argues that the transmission of affect changes the biochemistry and neurology of an individual; biology does not determine social life, but socially created affect can change our biology (also Crawford 2014). This is also called neuroplasticity: even the adult brain is plastic and changeable. In social neurology, which assumes that the social environment shapes the biology of an individual, neuroplasticity means that by observing the individual we can learn about collective emotions (Jeffery 2014). For International Relations, recognising that 'the personal is political,' means acknowledging that emotions are related to structures of power. Structures of power influence emotions and emotions can motivate the movements that change structures.

Emotions are felt and expressed through an interaction between biology, subjectivity and power. The prospect that emotional change encourages change in communities and society is an important premise of this study. As Swati Parashar (2011) argues, the emotions of the individual are not entirely controlled by power structures.

We perceive and sense our body emoting, and others' bodies emoting. The way in which emotion is a corporeal and interpersonal experience constitutes the basis for theorising a politics of emotion. Because this research analyses aesthetics, I can only learn about the bodymind of others through the aesthetics of the *object-body*; that is, a view from the outside. Through the aesthetic analysis I will not try to determine what someone is actually feeling (because this would be a mimetic reading), but what *appears* to be happening or what bodies seem to be doing.

As Colombetti (2014) writes, there are emotional expressions which are similar across cultures, independent of language. I try to address the difficulties of reading the body while still trying to read the body, because the body is there to be seen and I cannot close my eyes to it. Even though at times I emphasise the biological side of emotion, I am not saying that the human being can be reduced to neurobiology. I am equally curious about how the social moment influences different emotional worlds.

Although I rely on sensing the object-body in stories, images and sounds, my attempt is to show the importance of these lives for our political reality. And I do not end there. Text, film and music all act upon the spectator's body. Sharing stories of compassion *is* the politics of compassion. All the material presented here are acts upon the body, and hopefully will work to challenge our stubborn, often pessimistic, ways of thinking about human capacity. To enter the stories is to enter and imagine new worlds.

2

Condemned to Hope

In late 2014, I met Chechens living outside their homeland for the first time. Some were refugees, but not everyone. I first went to see a family in their home. The family's father was absent, and the mother greeted me warmly with an embrace. She did her prayers, and I exchanged some words with her daughter. Afterwards, we suddenly had to leave. I did not realise that we were about to witness a group of young Chechen women and girls performing in their traditional costumes. This performance was just for me, and I found myself seated in a chair alone in front of the young dancers. Later, because of my allergies, I had to decline a table full of cakes the women had prepared. I remembered reading about Chechen hospitality and felt ashamed. We talked about life, about dance, a disappeared brother, a search for a job, Chechen-only marriages, traditions and the fabric their dresses were made of.

We did not discuss war.

I hastily filmed some clips with my mobile phone. Among those clips was one of a young woman singing a song called *Daimohk*, meaning ancestral land. The song is about the beauty of nature and the Chechen landscape. It is also about honour and dignity, and love for the homeland. I did not get permission to publish the song because I had no contact with the singer. The missing song is a silence, a rupture, an empty soundscape. If I do find the singer and get permission, I will publish the song on my website. Research is a process.

Why Chechnya?

Chechnya is a republic of the Russian Federation in the North Caucasus with slightly over one million inhabitants, of which a majority are of Chechen descent. Massive war crimes took place in Chechnya during the two wars after the collapse of the Soviet Union, including rape, mutilation, torture, kidnapping and murder. The sweep operations conducted by Russian Special Forces and contract soldiers of the second war have been called a collective punishment aimed to destroy the cohesion of local communities (Gilligan 2010; Médecins Sans Frontières 1999).

When I began this research project in 2013, I wanted to find out how people could experience compassion in the context of war, and what forms compassion could take. I could have chosen any war as the context, but I was already working with Russian area studies for a decade and wanted to learn more about Chechnya. I do not have any personal connection to Chechnya or any exciting story to tell about how this research came about. I simply thought of Chechnya when I thought of war. Perhaps the fact that I do not speak or understand Russian well enough is one reason I began looking beyond words towards the body and aesthetics. My lack of language skills never prevented communication, and human-to-human bonding with the Chechens I had the privilege of meeting. In fact, with difficulties in language-based communication, the body stands out as the means with which to speak.

In this chapter I provide context for understanding the two wars in Chechnya, and I present an overview of some cultural aspects. The following chapters often refer to 'tradition,' not because time has stopped, but because the idea of tradition is the idea of community – the Chechen community tied to its war history, cultural history, land, customs and identity.

Aesthetics of Tradition

It is not an easy task to conduct research on Chechnya, especially for non-Russian and non-Chechen speakers (Jaimoukha 2005). Societies are constantly changing and the purpose of this book is not to generalise and categorise Chechens. As I will later explain, this means trying to avoid *stilling*. At the same time, I make visible these stills, which often relate to traditions like the clan system, honour, hospitality, Sufism, folklore and social structures. The emphasis on tradition, and the construction of Chechen people/identity as a singularity stills the Chechen community into a static and homogenous one. The purpose for this may be to build a sense of community for people living in the aftermath of war and genocide. The act of stilling the community is a survival strategy.

The narrative of Chechen tradition, including descriptions of that which is inherent, historical and shared in the community, is part of the aesthetics of Chechen war experience. There is no authentic Chechnya to be discovered, but there is an idea of the authentic which keeps surfacing in the material analysed here. The tension between the idea of maintaining Chechen tradition and the abandoning of tradition in war time is at the core of the politics of emotions in Chechnya. This is why the stories and images that are most interesting in terms of emotions are often related to traditions, and the patriarchal system which sustains them. I will explain some of the social structures to which the idea of Chechen identity and way of life are attached.

Amjad Jaimoukha (2005), who I refer to often in this chapter, explains the difficulties in describing social structures, such as the *tukhum-taip* system, because there is no stable model to present. Traditions are always changing. According to Jaimoukha (2005), clan exclusivity has become less pronounced, even though it still manifests in people seeking marriage outside the clan (*taip/teip*) but inside the tribe (*tukhum*). Kvedaravicius (2012) discusses the relationship of *teip* affinity to actual public governance in Chechnya, and writes that the discourse on *teip* affiliation is strong but the affiliation does not necessarily manifest in governance practices. How the *teip* system manifests in social relations is a question of social ties "forged and severed, politics enabled and forsaken, deaths occasioned or forestalled" (Kvedaravicius 2012: 181). In other words, "discourses perpetually linger on the verge of enactment within temporalities" (Kvedaravicius 2012: 181). There is no one story to tell about Chechnya, there are stories which are real as they become enacted, lived experiences. For example, the dichotomy between the local tradition of Sufi Islam and Wahhabism is enacted in the practise of the fight against terrorism. The local enforcers of anti-terror campaigns are amnestied rebels, former *Wahhabity* now fighting against *Wahhabism,* who can be accused of being *Wahhabity* themselves. Religious difference is sometimes entangled with blood feud sentiments, in which case revenge can be targeted against *Wahhabi* even if it originates in blood revenge.

For me the interest is in how traditions and 'anti-traditions' are aestheticised – how they are drawn as central to the everyday experience. Khassan Baiev (et al. 2003) refers to tradition – hospitality, respect for elders, honour, blood revenge, modesty, bravery – continuously as a way of explaining Chechnya to the foreign reader. But traditions are multifaceted too. For example, blood feud does not always lead to violence. The community deciding on the punishment can exercise forgiveness, requesting compensation for the victim's family. Baiev offers an example: a family that lost its son took in the perpetrator to their family as their surrogate son.

Tradition is an important discourse which constructs the collective identity of a people under attack. Traditions are under threat in war, and to practice and remember them is to hold on to the collectively defined self. To not refer to tradition, in this context, is interesting too. Milana Terloeva (2006), who I introduce in Chapter six, writes very little about marriage tradition or honour, for example, when she describes the loves and losses of her friends.

Although with regards to other themes, Terloeva too brings forth visions of Chechen mentality, spirit and tradition. I will argue that her writing, stripped of references to patriarchal traditions, is then a politics of love.

Like the autobiographies of Baiev (et al. 2003) and Terloeva (2006), the documentaries I analyse in this study bring forth ideas of tradition, or rather, they visualise and make them audible. It is no wonder that the Sufi ritual *zikr* has ended up in documentaries on Chechnya, because it is impressive and strange. *Zikr*, in which the participants are seeking a trance-like state, is made of synchronous movement and religious chanting. The soundscape of *zikr* is powerful even for the distant observer through the screen. Chechen dance, *lezginka*, discussed in Chapter four similarly exemplifies the importance of corporeal-aesthetic moves and rhythms of war/(post-)war experiences. In addition to the dance present in films, both Baiev (et al. 2003) and Terloeva (2006) write about wedding dance in their wartime memoires.

Jaimoukha (2005: 6–7) calls the Chechen struggle against Russian invasions and exportations a mechanism for "internalising history and propagating it through esoteric institutions." Thus, the *taip* (clan) system and Sufism act as a means to preserve Chechen-ness. To cover all the elements of Chechen society, history and institutions in this book would be impossible, but I make references in order to provide context for the analysis while trying to avoid distancing, exoticising and using a Western colonial gaze to describe a foreign culture. It is not the otherness I want to bring forth in this book, but rather the sameness. This sameness relates to a culture of violence and the stories that resonate across cultures and countries, but also to a culture of healing and resistance to violence – the important stories of survival. The experience of violence, be it war, intimate partner violence, sexual violence, psychological violence, abuse or other forms, induces similar expressions of trauma (Lewis Herman 2011). Individual trauma is connected to collective trauma. I believe that the investigation of emotions in war is related to experiences of violence and healing. A sensing and constant negotiation of difference is my solution to the ethics of researching the foreign and unfamiliar, or sometimes not so unfamiliar. I do not claim that bringing the research close to the skin is always better than other ways of researching, but I hope to give it a chance.

So Tired After the Wars

War history seems to be the most important history of Chechnya to tell. If you search for articles and books on Chechnya, you find war sooner rather than later. Constantly on guard, Chechens have fought invasions and tried to preserve their community. Even before encounters with Russia, in medieval times, Chechens fought hordes of Tatar-Mongols. When I interviewed two Chechen men living outside of Chechnya, they impressed me with their historical knowledge. At the same time, they told me how much of that history has been lost because "it is difficult to write and fight at the same time" (Ali and Said 2017). In fact, the wars destroyed much of the written history stored in Grozny (Tishkov 2004). But Ali and Said want to tell me about the fights against the Mongols. They tell me that Chechen warriors shaved their heads so that the Mongols could not hang the decapitated enemy heads by the hair while riding their horses. The story makes us three laugh. Even if I do not ask, we return to war all the time, sometimes joking, sometimes serious. It is present, waiting to be remembered, a historical memory not to be erased. But the women I met in Ali's house, and at the cultural centre where the young women danced for me, do not talk about the war with me.

The early nineteenth century Russian-Caucasian War, before Chechnya was part of Russia, was the bloody precedent of the post-Soviet era wars (Jaimoukha 2005). It involved deportations to Siberia, civilian killings, burnt villages and destroyed livelihoods. In 1861, Russia finally annexed Chechnya. This was also the period of Islamisation of the Chechen society when Imam Shamil came to the region and began converting the semi-pagan mountain Chechens. The end of the nineteenth century also saw the industrial exploitation of oil resources in Chechnya. 1917 presented the opportunity for independence, but in 1921 the Red Army occupied the North Caucasus. During the Soviet collectivisation policy, previous economic and social structures were ruptured. In 1934, Chechen and Ingush autonomic oblasts were combined as one, and, in 1936, made into an Autonomous Soviet Socialist Republic. When Germany invaded the Soviet Union in 1941, more than 30,000 Chechen and Ingush men enlisted in the Soviet Army, but volunteers also fought against the Red Army in the hope that Germany would liberate the North Caucasus.

In the winter of 1944, ethnic cleansing of Chechens and Ingush was implemented by Soviet troops. Masses were deported on Stalin's orders, in order to abolish Chechnya from the Soviet map. Jaimoukha (2005) describes how hundreds of thousands were herded to collection points and forced into trains for a trip that lasted days, and even weeks. At least one quarter perished during the trip or during the first months of exile. Russians, Ukranians and Daghestani resettled the Grozny Oblast. The deported were sent to Kazakhstan, Kirghizia, and elsewhere in the Soviet Union.

Milana Terloeva (2006) recounts her grandmother's experiences of deportation to Kazakhstan. They were chased out of their houses on the night of February 23, 1944. Her grandmother was with her siblings, cousins, mother and grandfather who refused to leave. Those who stayed were killed, even burnt alive. In 1957, when they were allowed to return after 13 years of exile, they had no homes to return to. Russians had taken over, and they could not return to the mountains but were forced to live in the capital Grozny. They would rebuild and take back their lands, Terloeva's grandmother explains to her, only for everything to be destroyed again. And when the second war was ongoing, when everything had been destroyed again, her grandmother comforted her, saying "we will rebuild, like always." She continued, "You have no right to despair. We are condemned to hope, Milana." To be condemned means to be punished by an external force. To be condemned *to hope* is a choice, it is the determination to survive the punishment. *Condemned to hope* is an expression which captures the lived experience of Terloeva's grandmother. It is a reminder to future generations that they could live without hope, but they would not rebuild or heal without it.

After the exile, the population more than doubled over a 30 year period, and Chechen nationalism became more assertive in the 1980s, in particular with *perestroika* and *glasnost* which allowed more freedom of expression (Jaimoukha 2005). The wars which followed, in 1994 and 1999 were not only fought for political survival, but also for cultural identity and heritage, material and non-material. In October 1991, Dzhokhar Dudayev won the presidency, and soon after issued a degree proclaiming state sovereignty seceding Chechnya from Russia which caused Boris Yeltsin to declare a state of emergency in Chechnya. In 1992, Ingush districts separated from Chechnya. After Russian attempts to support Chechen opposition to bring Dudayev down failed in December 1994, Yeltsin sent in troops.

Russian troops met fierce resistance on New Year's Eve in the city of Grozny. The civilian population was trapped in Grozny where apartment buildings were targeted (Gilligan 2010). According to Jaimoukha (2005), the Russian strategy was to terrorise the population by massacring civilians. Anna Politkovskaya (2003) describes the famous fight over Grozny as the spectacular slaughter of the Russian forces. According to Politkovskaya, the first generation of Chechen fighters were volunteers who were not motivated only by the present but by the past as well – they fought for their ancestors who perished in 1944 as well as those who died fighting Russia even before that. The second war made many of these young men professionals. Warlord Shamil Basayev attracted many of the former fighters, and they turned to Islamic revolution in order to fight foreign domination. But, as Politkovskaya explains, it was not Islamic tradition but rather the violent chaos of various private armies seeking sources of income in the ruined country that encouraged the religious aspect in the second war.

31 *Sounds of War*

President Dudayev was killed by a Russian rocket in April 1996. Presidential elections were approaching in Russia and Yeltsin needed good news. Russian troops were unprepared and the invasion ended in a standstill forcing Moscow to negotiate a cease-fire in the Spring of 1996. After Chechen forces stormed Grozny, causing heavy losses to Russian troops, a peace treaty was finally signed on August 31st. Aslan Maskhadov was elected president in January 1997 and in May he signed an agreement with Yeltsin for the future of Chechnya.

Moscow's hardliners considered Chechnya a bandit state and wanted to reverse the peace agreement. Military humiliation, the Caspian oil pipeline passing through Chechnya, and the dangerous example of national ambitions were motivations for the next invasion. Chechnya was in internal chaos and the economy was crushed with high unemployment. There were problems such as lawlessness, an industry of kidnappings, an illegal oil trade, and rivalling warlords with their militias consolidating their power through violence (Jaimoukha 2005; see also Russell 2007).

The second war was preceded by the Chechen rebel Shamil Basayev sending his army to Dagestan in support of separatist rebels. As another incentive to use force, the apartment building bombing of September 1999 was blamed on a Chechen terrorist. Afterwards, Prime Minister Vladimir Putin ordered air bombings of Grozny, followed by a land invasion. Putin's rise to popularity and finally presidency in March 2000 has been linked to the politics around the war in Chechnya, and the apartment bombings in Moscow and other cities in Autumn 1999 (Russell 2007).

The Putin administration framed the war as a fight against Islamic extremism. The second war brought a more explicitly religious connotation, and along with it the accusation that Chechens were involved in international terrorism through *Wahhabite* militarism. Wahhabism (a radical religious-political doctrine) was introduced in Chechnya in the early 1990s (Kvedaravicius 2012). According to Johnston (2008), foreign Islamists meant resources, skills, recruits, and money for the Chechen resistance. It was in Russia's interest to frame the war as an operation to eliminate international terrorism rather than an armed conflict between Russia and Chechnya. Such framing excluded other knowledge, history and experiences from the narrative.

The war left one third of the Chechen population displaced, as some forty towns and villages were bombed (Gilligan 2010). Chechen fighters committed crimes as well. According to Human Rights Watch (2000), the fighters put civilians at risk and beat and killed village elders who tried to stop the fighters entering their village. They also committed kidnappings during the interwar years, and were responsible for hostage-takings and suicide bombings against Russian civilians (see Gilligan 2010). And Russian soldiers cannot be lumped into one category as perpetrators, either. As Gilligan (2010) explains, conscripted soldiers had lower moral due to their own mistreatment and the brutality of the war, which sometimes led to their reluctance to participate. Maya Eichler (2011), who interviewed Russian veterans of the Chechen wars, discovered men who were morally opposed to and unprepared for the war. One of her interviewees, who led troops to Grozny in 1994, considered the war politically motivated and unjust. He considered Chechens his fellow citizens. Soldiers used excessive force and sexual violence against civilians but war crimes charges were never brought forward and only a few cases were prosecuted in Russia.

Western states did not intervene, and could do nothing to prevent the human suffering in Chechnya. Many saw the war as Russia's internal matter. Putin was elected president of the Russian Federation and Akhmad Kadyrov, who fought against Russia but changed sides, was appointed head of the Chechen administration in June 2000. In 2002, when Chechen fighters took hostages in the Dubrovka Theatre in Moscow and the Russian military pumped poisonous gas into the ventilation system killing over 200 hostages and 41 Chechen fighters, Putin's line hardened against Chechnya and he refused negotiations with Maskhadov. According to Russell (2007), since Dubrovka, or even since 2000, Putin's solution was the 'Chechenisation' of the conflict; that is, he chose to transfer the fight against secessionism and terrorism to pro-Moscow Chechens under Kadyrov's leadership. In October 2003, Kadyrov was elected president but he was assassinated in May 2004. Again, the war destroyed economic enterprises and infrastructures such as transport systems, and electricity supply utilities were severely damaged. Moreover, the two wars have been environmental catastrophes due to oil spillages, illegal oil refineries and water pollution, while landmines and disease have caused further suffering. According to Jaimoukha (2005) the economy reverted back to agriculture and cattle-breeding when restoration funds did not reach the population.

Russia took over Grozny in early 2000, but the war did not end when the full-scale offensive did. Chechnya was established as a Counter-Terrorist Zone which actually produced terrorism by allowing violence, torture and kidnapping (see Kvedaravicius 2012). There is no data available on the number of deaths in the two wars, but according to Gilligan, the most reliable figures are between 65,000–75,000 (2010: 3). Moreover, several thousand went missing after the 'cleansings' (Laurén 2009). Abductions by federal forces were a business in which the abducted were sold back alive or dead to their families. Russian prison camps were sites of systematic and large-scale torture. The war did not destroy the lives of Chechens only. According to

Russell (2007), a large proportion of the million and a half Russian troops suffered from posttraumatic stress, which is commonly called the 'Chechen syndrome.'

In 2007, Ramzan Kadyrov became president after the death of his father. Kadyrov has Putin's support even as I write this, and Chechnya has received significant financial support from Moscow. The majority religion in Chechnya is Islam with two branches, canonical Sunni, represented by the Shafii legal school, and Sufism. President Kadyrov has been promoting a peculiar mixture of the two as part of a new Chechen identity. Kadyrov has his own private militia called *Kadyrovtsy* inherited from his father's security force.

After the war, Chechnya remained a Counter-Terrorist Zone until 2009. Violence was "lingering heavily on the spectacle of reconstructed cities and the subsidized economy" (Kvedaravicius 2012: 7). It meant the same methods as in war time: aerial bombardments, the wiping out of villages, the killing of civilians, concentration camps and torture chambers. Violence also created financial opportunities such as kidnappings for ransom, bribes at checkpoints, illegal oil and weapons trades and so forth. By 2006, as Kvedaravicius (2012) notes, the operation involved over 45,000 federal troops, thousands of law enforcement and security service agents under federal control, and thousands of Chechen soldiers and law enforcement agents. Forced disappearances became widespread and systematic cons-tituting crimes against humanity as thousands have disappeared, most of them young men, since 1999 (Human Rights Watch 2005; Gilligan 2010).

Pro-Moscow Chechen forces gradually took over the task of abductions from the federal troops. The operation relied on local Chechen factions and groups around the families of former field commanders who had changed to the federal side. The Russian human rights organisation *Memorial* kept a database of the disappeared and had an office in Chechnya until July 2009 when Natalia Estemirova was abducted and killed. Some people have chosen not to report the disappearances, fearing further persecution. Disappearances and killings, reportedly targeting sexual minorities, continue to date (Hille 2015; Mirovalev 2015; Walker 2017). Yulia Gorbunova (2017) from Human Rights Watch writes how asylum seekers from the North Caucasus, especially Chechnya, have arrived at the Belarus-Polish border hoping to cross to safety. In the summer of 2016, some 400–800 people, most of whom were from Chechnya, tried to cross the border from Brest to Terespol. They were escaping the violence of the Kadyrov regime in fear for their lives.

Kvedaravicius explains that, as a result of the abductions, terrorists were simultaneously produced and destroyed: people changed sides when security and financial interests were at stake. Different agents, groups and institutions were in abundance in the counter-terrorist zone. "Thus, military battalions, combat units and institutions with strange acronyms, and special groups, police stations, prosecutors' offices, and courthouses [...] were now vying and collaborating in the production of terrorists while other, complex, post-war entanglements were weighing upon them" (Kvedaravicius 2012: 14). Kvedaravicius argues that there is no post-war situation in Chechnya because violence continues to permeate the everyday.

As Kvedaravicius shows through his study and the film *Barzakh*, which I analyse in Chapter four, war continues to be lived and experienced long after the bombs stop falling. Crawford (2015) explains that if war is seen through the logic of rational thinking, and not emotions, it leads to war being defined by the number of casualties – war calculable and quantifiable. But if we look at emotions in war, we see war creeping in, affecting people in diverse ways, and staying for way too long. We have a much longer timeline and many more variables. We see that emotions are constitutive of war and politics. It is for this reason that we need to remain interested in Chechnya even if nothing dramatic seems to be happening there (see Nivat 2001).

A Chechen man I met in 2017 told me about the climate in Chechnya at that time. It was a difficult decision to include our conversation in this book, because talking about politics in Chechnya is a risk for Chechens in the diaspora as much as for those living in Chechnya. For many, the political climate in Chechnya has gotten worse than it was during the war with Russia because now Chechens have been betrayed from the inside. The documentarist Monan Loizeau, in an interview she gave about her film on (post-)war Chechnya, says that the enemy used to be only Russia; now, in the face of Kadyrov's terror, people are afraid of being betrayed by their own family because solidarity no longer exists (Tchernookova 2015). For those who dare to voice their criticism against Kadyrov's regime, the result can be death. The man's daughter came into the room and said: "It's a crazy country. You know, here on the street you can say anything you like. But not there." The Chechenisation of the second war made Chechens turn against each other, and silenced the people. "Kadyrov betrayed us," the man said. He does not even believe Kadyrov is a real Chechen. For him, Kadyrov is a showman, Russia's puppet, and the rebuilt Grozny is a facade which does not concern the majority of people who live in poverty. "This is a big test for us. I trust God," he sighed.

The Chechen man talked about the lack of freedom that is embodied in the danger that comes with growing a beard. As a legacy of the Chechenisation and the anti-terrorist campaign of the second war, beards provoke suspicion.

"The bearded men are considered Wahhabi," he said. This is how war continues as a lived, bodily experience.

I ask if two Chechen men would like to return home. "No," they answered, because there is no normal life anymore. "You are either with him or against him [Kadyrov]. There is no return for those who oppose his policies," the other man said. "We are attached to our land, our hearts are always there," he continued. It is not an easy decision for them to live abroad, but it would be worse in Chechnya. The punishment for criticising the regime would fall upon the family, the relatives, and the entire tribe. It is because of an anti-terror law, the men told me. "Everyone is so tired after the wars."

To Stay Humane

War can be statistics. It can be the count of dead civilians and soldiers. It can be the number of injured or disappeared, the number of babies born with disabilities, or how many people suffer from trauma or mental illness. It can be a report on human rights violations. It can be a description of military strategy, or events unfolding on the battlefield. A description of war can include numbers of arms and tanks or how many cities were destroyed. A description of war can include information on the resulting natural disasters or the destruction of infrastructure. A description of war could include details about how people suffered from hunger, lack of health care, education, or housing. Causes and effects of war could be explained by religion, corruption, historical legacy, oil, economy, greed, hate, identity, and the mountains of Chechnya.

Chechen war history often places genocide and Russian cruelty or the heroic warrior tradition at the centre (see Akhmadov and Lanskoy 2010; Jaimoukha 2005). Such war histories tell of conquering Russians and fighting Chechens, but they tell little about the strategies, hopes, and experiences of civilians in wartime. It has been the work of human rights activists to collect testimonials validating the suffering of ordinary people or the destruction of livelihoods and nature. Médecins Sans Frontières has also done important work collecting testimonials in Chechnya (for example, Médecins Sans Frontières 2014) as has Memorial. The French journalist Anne Nivat (2001) travelled illegally across the war zone, covering the second war and people's experiences, reporting with great risk through a satellite phone she had to strap to her belly. The human rights activist and journalist Anna Politkovskaya, who was murdered in 2006, became a witness to the second war, and her description of war in *A Small Corner of Hell: Dispatches from Chechnya* (2003) also focuses on testimonials. As Derluguian (2003) writes, reading this book, which portrays the complexity of the human condition, requires moral labour.

The moral labour comes from the connections the reader forms to the stories of individuals touched by war. The reader becomes a witness of war, even if a distant one.

I am interested in war as lived experience, "and that means looking at social aspects of war, people and/in/as war, rather than subsuming them in causes and effects" (Sylvester 2013a: 671). For me, this means embarking on a path which takes from and develops further research on *emotions* and *lived experience* (for example, Brennan 2004; Butler 2009; Penttinen 2013; Sylvester 2013b). Thus, I am preoccupied with war in the sense that it touches people's lives (Sylvester 2011; Butler 2009). As the ethnomusicologist Martin Daughtry (2015: 26) puts it, "armed violence, through its sensory and affective intensity, brings injury to a far larger population than those whose bodies are penetrated by flying metal." I believe embodied emotions are stories that make us deconstruct and rethink our knowledge about people in wartime. Thus I chose to look at something less obvious: the emotion of compassion, the role of children, and finally, love in war.

In this study, I take the everyday to be a site of resistance, resistance which manifests in compassion. By resistance, I mean material bodies that refuse to become firmly and unambiguously located in systems of power (Väyrynen et al. 2016). Encounters are sites of resistance, and can be mundane. Furthermore, they note that the corporeal and gestural body politic may sometimes appear as being without clear purpose and direction yet different struggles and everyday relations of bodies evoke various capacities and potentialities which pave the way for political agency. The stories I share here, and the readings of the body I make are founded upon this same idea of mundane choreographies which are unstable, almost invisible or unfitting, and seem to refuse to be stilled.

People are never fully governed. They are not just passive victims to be rescued, or else it would be a hopeless life (Banes 2015). In the course of this research I have become curious about the dichotomy of victim/perpetrator. This is problematic when the two are made categories which exclude each other, and these categories are seen to define human nature. The reason why it is important to discuss, not so much abandon, the victim/perpetrator divide is that in a culture of violence, we need to think about how to prevent violence, which means getting at the root of violence in human experience. A man who is a *victim* of war can also be a *perpetrator* of violence by participating in a bride kidnap, blood revenge or honour killing. That same person can carry the trauma of Stalin's deportation, and is also a *victim* of the patriarchal culture which encourages and normalises violence against women and sexual minorities. Thus, there might be no single narrative to tell.

A compassionate encounter between perpetrator and victim can be an act of everyday resistance to cruelty in war (Hast 2014). Politkovskaya (2003) shares a story of Rosita, who was held in a tiny pit for twelve days, and tortured with electric shocks. There was a soldier who one night threw her a piece of carpet. Her release was promised in exchange for a ransom so big the villagers could not afford it. Eventually the soldiers (Federal Security Servicemen) settled for a tenth of the sum and Rosita was released. The practise Politkovskaya (2003: 49) describes here is "a concentration camp with a commercial streak." But this concentration camp had a soldier who offered a piece of carpet which led Rosita to realise the soldier is a human being too.

Politkovskaya, travelling in Chechnya, witnessed the destruction of the human spirit. For example, many Russian elderly were abandoned in Grozny during the wars. Politkovskaya was at the backyard of a former food factory in Shali, Chechnya, where she witnessed hundreds of homeless refugees cursing and fighting with each other while in queue for a food ration from the Russian government. She (2003: 43) writes, "This is an utter loss of human feeling, total alienation. It's impossible not to notice the extent to which traditional Chechen mentality has been destroyed here."

For all she witnessed in Chechnya, Politkovskaya (2003: 111) concluded that, "Wherever cruelty is a norm of life, no one can expect compassion and mercy, not even the weakest." Compassion in war is not to be taken for granted. Yet, compassion is not absent in a war zone, or when post-war begins to emerge. Compassion in war is human revolution, perhaps the most profound revolution possible. The presence of compassion in a war torn society, among people deprived of everything, is what we need to learn about because it enrichens our understanding of how war is experienced in relation to the most profound human (and non-human) connections and bonds. As Penttinen (2013) writes, research does not always have to analyse the disease, it can also look into the cure which is found in the human being herself. Compassion can be a cure, and I will argue later in this chapter that love can be a cure too. But first I need to explain what compassion is about, and why I am interested in its embodiment.

3

Pit

Alone in the pit, in the dark, in the woods
Alone in the pit, in the dark, in the woods
Alone in the pit, in the dark, in the woods
Alone in the pit, in the dark, in the woods

Seek the salvation
Look, not to the light
But, in to the eyes of the stranger
To the friend
You don't know
Why he's here
But he is
And he takes
And he holds
And he saves

Alone in the pit, in the dark, in the woods
Alone in the pit, in the dark, in the woods
Alone in the pit, in the dark, in the woods
Alone in the pit, in the dark, in the woods

Pit was the very first song. I wrote it in the winter of 2004 after I listened to an audio recording of *The Oath: A Surgeon Under Fire* by the Chechen surgeon Khassan Baiev (et al. 2003). There was one story which ran through my spine and froze my body into listening carefully: Baiev was kept in a pit after being accused of helping a Russian doctor escape. Amazed by the story, I wrote *Pit* in one go, with a very clear melody pumping through me. Baiev was a plastic surgeon, who got his education in a medical school in Siberia. But during the war he had to perform all types of procedures in the hardest of conditions. As a doctor, Baiev could use his hands to save lives, and his hands embodied his compassion. But Baiev was also saved several times himself, often almost as if by a miracle. To me it seemed like compassion was returning to him in the form of strangers who saved his life. This is what the song is about. We have done different versions of this song, and Baiev himself has listened to at least one version commenting "sounds great" via Twitter. This book includes the acoustic version, in which I play one of the guitars.

When Baiev was young he spent summers in Makazhoi. There his father told him and his brother Hussein stories about their ancestors and clan, or *teip* which consisted of some 100 families, about the deportations and stories of blood feud. The memories of those stories and the beauty of the mountains would sustain him later during the darkest moments of his life. "I still see those two black eagles soaring in the sky, and a shiver runs down my spine" he says (Baiev et al. 2003: 41–2).

Vulnerable Compassion

All too often compassion is taken for granted, and that leads to lack of vision in terms of how compassion is emoted in the body, and how compassion can manifest. Goetz et al. (2010) argue that, as an emotion, compassion can be grouped with love, tenderness and caring, but due to its social nature it is a separate emotion. The authors emphasise the separation of compassion from the emotions of fear and sorrow; yet, it does not mean that compassion and sorrow could not alternate or mix in the emotional experience. Compassion is often used interchangeably with empathy, and it is hard to say where compassion ends and empathy begins, or vice versa. For Goetz et al. (2010), empathy signifies a capacity to recognise the other's emotions while sympathy signifies feeling with somebody else. Brené Brown (2012) sees sympathy as feeling *for* and empathy as feeling *with*. In this case, sympathy is a shame trigger because it signals that the one feeling sympathy is somehow better than the other. In fact, according to Brown (2012), shame resilience is all about empathy. Sympathy, instead, resembles pity. Emma Hutchison (2014) aptly describes pity as a top-down approach to aid in her study on images from the tsunami that hit Asia in 2004 – pity is based on inequality and is thus problematic.

Compassion is often conceptualised as recognition of the other's suffering and the wish to alleviate it – an emotion with an action tendency (Goetz et al. 2010; Ure and Frost 2014). But I argue that there can be compassionate action without conscious feeling of compassion, and compassion without a specific action tendency. Moreover, since emotions are a crucial part of perceiving the self, compassion plays a part in the construction of the self as the individual moves and relates to others in the world. This means that instead of looking at compassion only as directed outside (as empathy or the need to alleviate others' suffering), compassion is integral to the constant becoming of the self.

Even if action tendency is a rather popular way to conceptualise compassion, Brown's (2012) way of separating empathy from compassion is more convincing: whereas empathy is a skill set, compassion signifies a deep spiritual belief about how to live life. For Brown, compassion is a relationship between equals, not a relationship between the wounded and the healed. As such, compassion is more like a *state of life*, but still, like other emotions it is triggered by internal and external stimuli, experienced in the bodymind with varying intensity. Compassion as state of life can be explained through the parable of *Bodhisattva Never Disparaging*, from *The Lotus Sutra*, in which the Bodhisattva greets everyone humbly and is slandered because of his conviction to treat everyone as an equal (266–268). Bowing to everyone, his compassionate movement in the world represents this deep spiritual belief about how to live life. The *Bodhisattva* demonstrates respect towards others and bows even to those who beat him. Bowing is then his visibly manifest action tendency of compassion. He eventually turns the slanderers into supporters. In the parable there is no separation between the victim (with no agency) and the compassionate party (with agency) – or the healed and the wounded – but there are people who choose to behave in a certain way towards others. The Bodhisattva does not discriminate between those who do and do not deserve his compassion. Pity is not part of the Bodhisattva's model because when pity is evoked a sense of superiority manifests. The Bodhisattva does not select those worthy of his compassion, nor does he seek revenge upon the wrongdoers.

The Bodhisattva way of compassion is related to spirituality. What I mean by spirituality is a strong belief in the connection between lives and a sensing of the world in terms of deeper structures than political or economic. Spirituality can be about faith in laws (of life, of God, of tradition) but encompasses an open-ness, a sensitivity, a vulnerability. The Bodhisattva was not praised for his behaviour. He was not rewarded and thanked. By bowing to everyone without exception, he pushed the boundaries of appropriate conduct and was persecuted. The point is not in imagining a person whose compassion is of such magnitude he can tolerate all kinds of abuse, but to theorise a view of compassion which departs from spirituality, a sense of connection to life around us.

Compassion is tied together with vulnerability. Vulnerability is the prerequisite for social relationships. Vulnerability enables both hurt and compassion. As Judith Butler (2004) writes, the body implies mortality, vulnerability and agency, and it has a private and public dimension. The body is exposed to gazes, touch and violence; and the body is at risk of being the instrument of all this. The vulnerable body is of the essence to studies on violence and war experience. Bodies which are violated in so many ways in war are the vulnerable bodies. In the media, these are often female bodies and children's bodies; they are dead bodies or mutilated bodies. At the least, they are visibly suffering bodies: traumatised, sad, scared, tired, hungry and so forth. The more we see the vulnerability of the body, the more real war becomes to us and – as it is assumed in the logic of humanitarian reason – the more we feel for the distant others.

But I propose a complementary perspective: vulnerability as openness to the world. A person who is frail yet not weak – one who possesses a sense of agency while being acutely aware of life's fragility. Adopting from Brown (2012), being vulnerable means being willing to be seen by others. For Brown (2012), vulnerability is the starting point of many positive emotions, and she further argues that without vulnerability there is no empathy. I would continue that compassion is the willingness to be seen by others and *to see others as well*. Vulnerability takes courage because it entails a risk: there is something, often much, to lose. In war or in a repressive or violent environment/relation-ship, the risk and potential harm is even greater. Thus, the vulnerable body is twofold. One side is the victim, exposed and hurt. The other side is the same vulnerable body, the same precarious life, but active, not passive, in the war and (post-)war contexts. Still exposed, still hurt, but letting people come close. In Later, I will discuss how Khassan Baiev (et al. 2003) redefined his openness and what it means for him to be an honourable Chechen man by writing about his personal life and emotions, and sharing his intimate secrets.

Performative Compassion

Often, compassion is seen as a potential model of moral behaviour – a political virtue. If compassion is trainable, as Martha Nussbaum (2003) sees it, it is not merely a corporeal sensation. Compassion is also a moral choice and not simply a natural reaction to suffering (Von Dietze and Orb 2000). But according to Nussbaum, some are sceptical of compassion's virtues because they see it as too ambiguous, too unequal, too narrow. Compassion can lead to victimisation and inequality just like it can be a route to solidarity. Julia Welland (2015) is likewise critical of compassion when discussing soldiering. She writes that compassion is an emotion which can obscure and divert attention, separate and divide. She problematises soldiers' experiences of compassion in relation to the acts of violence they commit and celebrate. Compassion seems to comfort the soldiers, and it becomes a way for them to feel good about themselves. Welland argues that announcement of comp-assion can conceal the ongoing violence and obscenity of war. The first problem here is a lack of consideration for the soldiers' possible traumas (see

Van der Kolk 2014), and the second is a reading of compassion that is merely discursive and performative.

Welland (2015) calls compassion seductive and performative, as it works as an announcement of one's own virtue. Compassion can be viewed as a political/performative act, but such a view comes from the idea of emotions as disembodied – emotions as the mind's creations and property. We are no longer interested in how the person emotes and feels, but only with the construction of stories. The problem here is the linear causality drawn between emotion and action tendencies. A self-serving discourse on compassion is not the same as the *emotion* of compassion (the felt body state). It is not necessarily compassion at all which drives a soldier to find comfort in *thinking* about compassion as part of the self – one has now entered the world of ideas.

The third problem is that the divisions Welland refers to do not come from compassion as such but compassion entangled with other emotions, like anger or resentment, lack of compassion, pity or shame. Feelings of shame can be the trigger for performing compassion. Emotions can be, and are, performative, but they are more than that, because the bodymind is more than the conscious part of it: it entails automatic and non-conscious processes alike. This is why I do not analyse how people proclaim themselves as compassionate in their actions, but rather, I try to follow the stories and images of bodies in movement, which I believe take the researcher more toward the difficult terrain of emoting than the stories of and for the self.

Lauren Berlant (2004: 1) writes, "There is nothing clear about compassion except that it implies a social relation between spectators and sufferers, with the emphasis on the spectator's experience of feeling compassion and its subsequent relation to material practice." I have a different conceptualisation of compassion, one not based on a division between spectator and sufferer. I also challenge any linear relationship of compassion to material practice. The more we turn away from a narrow definition of compassion, the more deeply we need to look for the embodied, material and spiritual manifestations of it. Rather than taking compassion as a social and aesthetic technology of belonging (Berlant 2004), I am interested in it as an emotion related to a deep spiritual belief about how to live life which arises in the body. This approach sees compassion as the cure rather than the disease because it is based on the embodied view of compassion, the kinaesthetic exchange between bodies. It also allows us to incorporate many different acts and sensations of compassion, for example, the art of asking. Asking for help is at once courageous, vulnerable and compassionate because it allows the other person to be generous, to help and to feel compassion as well.

Body Creates the Lived Political

> The body does not move *into* space and time, it *creates* space
> and time: there is no space and time before movement
> (Manning 2007: xiii, emphasis in the original).

In early attachment between a parent and a child, touch is important. A child
seeks physical contact and cuddling, and the caretaker provides it spon-
taneously. As the author and activist Eve Ensler (2013: 1) writes, "A mother's
body against a child's body makes a place. It says you are here. Without this
body against your body there is no place." Without a body against a body,
there is no place. It is between bodies where politics takes place, too.

The lived political is the lived body, something we experience in daily life
rather than politics as out there within institutions or processes outside our
embodied reality. What is so political about the body is how, like Manning
eloquently writes, bodies create space and time by moving in it. The political
emerges as the body nudges, rushes, falls or gets up. The space changes
when a body enters it, or when the body leaves. The body's presence is
always temporary, there can be only visits. The everyday is a stage too, and
war is a stage on which the victim's body is violated, often resulting in trauma.
Trauma changes the body – trauma is physiological as much as it is
psychological. Bessel Van der Kolk (2014) writes that the entire body
responds to trauma, thus the act of telling one's story is usually not enough to
help the individual suffering from trauma. The hyper-vigilant body needs to
learn that the danger has passed. Trauma changes how mind and body
manage perceptions, not only how we think and what we think about but also
"our very capacity to think" (Van der Kolk 2014: Chapter two). When a person
manages to escape the danger, she regains her senses. But when one is
unable to escape, the brain continues producing stress chemicals, thus the
body keeps sending signals of danger even when danger has passed. For the
victim's sense of agency, the experience of having escaped is important for
the healing process. In Chapter five, I discuss how children express agency
as survivors making sense of a traumatic event. These children were trapped
for several days, witnessed the deaths of friends and family members, but
found their way out alive.

Attending to and acknowledging the body in all its visceral dimensions – the
experiential knowledge – is essential for being in charge of one's life and for
healing (Van der Kolk 2014). Peter A. Levine and Ann Frederick (1997) write
that trauma has long been considered a psychological and medical disorder
of the mind that ignores the two-way communication between body and mind
recently discovered by neuroscience. The vulnerable body in war is often

traumatised and thus disconnected. As Van der Kolk (2014) argues, trauma makes intimate relationships difficult, limits the imagination, brings numbness, traps and immobilises the person in fear, and often involves shame of what one did or did not do. But vulnerability's other side is that it entails the possibility of connection. The focus of this research is more on the healing and coping emotional-corporeal being, than in the causes and effects of trauma. The interest is in the aesthetics of vulnerability which bring forth embodied human connections. This necessitates directing the gaze from the suffering body to the possibilities of agency and positive emotions in war.

According to Damasio (2010), social emotions, as they appear to be dependent on education and the environment, seem like only a cognitive layer on the brain's surface. But compassion is more about the body than we might think. For one, the brain can simulate within its somatosensory regions certain body states as if they were occurring. Thus, even before an emotional change of body state actually occurs, the brain can produce a simulation of it. This simulation does not concern the body of oneself only, but the bodies of others too. For Damasio, in this capacity to simulate lies the neurological basis of empathy. In the 1990's empathy became associated with the so called mirror neurons, which were revealed by studying the neural activity in the brains of macaque monkeys. The mirror neurons, involved in motor control, were activated also when observing another monkey execute an action (Rizzolatti and Craighero 2004; Saarela et al. 2007; Kalat 2008). It is likely that mirror neurons exist also in the human brain; however, there is no conclusive proof of that to date. Yet, there is research to prove the existence of a neural basis of empathy, in other words, an overlap of neural activation between the self and the other (von Scheve and Salmela 2014).

Damasio explains that neurons in areas engaged with emotions activate regions which map body states and make the body move. Damasio (2010: 104) continues,

> As we witness an action in another, our body-sensing brain adopts the body state we would assume were we ourselves moving, and it does so, in all probability, not by passive sensory patterns but by a preactivation of motor structures – ready for action but not allowed to act yet – and in some cases by actual motor activation.

For Damasio, the capacity to simulate one's own body state is the reason why it is possible to simulate the other's. If pity is the feeling of emotion in which the suffering party is separate from the one feeling pity (see Hutchison 2014), then compassion is something that connects, and that connection is in the flesh and more precisely, "the actions with which we can portray the movements of others" (Damasio 2010: 257–8). Hayes and Tipper (2012) have shown in clinical studies how the fluency of motor actions evokes positive emotions. They argue that rather than emotions evoking motor responses, motor action (also observing motor action) evokes emotions. Yet the process of simulating the body state of the other is not just a mechanical activation of motor representations in the brain, it conveys meanings, that is, an understanding through the body (see Gaensbauer 2011).

Colombetti (2014), adopting the concept from the philosophy of Husserl, suggests that empathy is about feeling the other's lived body (*Leib*) – an experiential access to the other's subjectivity rather than merely seeing the other as a physical thing or a material object (*Körper*). Thompson (2007) explains that experience cannot be disclosed in its original first-person subjectivity from the second-person perspective of empathy. That is, the feeling is not primordially and bodily there, although the feeling can be remembered and imagined. To be more precise, in empathy we do not experience the other's body directly as our own body nor do we merely observe the other body. Even bodies through the screen, or in pictures and stories, excite our bodies (von Scheve and Salmela 2014). A person experiences kinaesthetic sensations while observing the activation of another body. This is not fusion but accompaniment (D'Aloia 2012), because I do not feel the other's sensations as my own (Colombetti 2014). I do feel them, but not as my subjectivity – my lived body – but as the other person's subjectivity.

Even though I am not researching the neural correlates of compassion, the neuroscientific findings prove the need to conceptualise compassion as a corporeal connection between individuals as much as a conscious feeling of an emotion. It is the bodymind at work, and it does not discriminate between bodily and mental experiences either conscious or non-conscious. Compassion is not co-passion, but involves identifying suffering as suffering, acknowledging its existence in another being and being a witness to it. By witnessing and validating, one makes the other's experience real. Next, I analyse three different war experiences related to compassion. First, a perspective on compassion which includes non-human embodiment; second, compassion through active engagement with emotions; third, compassion embodied in self-sacrifice. These experiences attest to the complexity of how compassion affects, and potentially hurts, bodies.

Dr. Baiev and the Cow Zoyka

Jane Goodall, the famous British anthropologist, ethnologist and primatologist who spent her career studying chimpanzees in Tanzania, says that if the emotions of pity and guilt are the reasons why we help someone, we are doing it for our own sake, to alleviate our own suffering. Goodall addresses empathy, which she experienced towards the chimpanzees she studied, and in fact, empathy enabled her to collect all that information about them. She also observed the social bonds between the chimpanzees and gathered evidence of love, altruism and empathy among the animals (Goodall and Berman 2000).

Related to stilling and categorisation which I discussed in Chapter one, Goodall writes, "Once we have labelled the things around us we do not bother to look at them carefully. Words are part of our rational selves, and to abandon them for a while is to give freer rein to our intuitive selves" (Goodall and Berman 2000: 79). Goodall was in the forest, enchanted by the rich sounds of the environment, and by all that she perceived around her. She experienced awareness, cessation of the voice within, a return to something forgotten and wonderful. For Goodall, animals and nature have a subject body and for a moment she refuses to use language to capture it.

War touches non-humans too, and, according to enactivism, life is always minded or mindful, and mind always shares the organisational properties of life. This means that there is life-mind continuity in living beings. The richer the living form, the richer the life (Colombetti 2012). To bridge the gap between life forms with a highly developed mind and other life forms is also to bridge the gap between mind and body. Enactivism is a post-humanist mindset but also a non-fragmented view of the organism. Animals are present in war too, yet we do not hear so much about them. Penttinen (2013) has challenged the idea of animals as objects, instead of subjects, in war, and argues that non-humans also participate in making the world known. She also questions the notion of knowing associated only with a thinking mind. I became interested in non-human war experience, although from a human point of view, after reading Baiev's encounter with the cow Zoyka (Baiev et al. 2003).

A woman came to Baiev's hospital begging for help. It was Malika Umazhova, whom Baiev recognised as a woman who was known for organising protests and talking back to the Russians. Umazhova (they called her by the last name) said a member of her family had been wounded. Umazhova said: "She's like a daughter to me," but she was embarrassed to say the family member was a cow. Baiev insisted he had no time to operate on animals, he had so many patients already. Umazhova begged for help. Cows were important for a Chechen family, so he finally agreed to go to their house. Nearly all houses on the way were damaged or ruined.

Zoyka, the cow, lay on her side and Umazhova began stroking the cow's head to comfort her. Baiev wanted to tie the animal's legs for the operation, but Umazhova says it is not necessary because Zoyka understands everything, and then says to the cow, "You understand, Doctor is here to make you better." Baiev anaesthetises the area of the wound and pulls a sharp piece of metal from the cow's neck. He was amazed that the entire operation, one and a half hours, the cow remained calm. The woman had five children, and they would be able to get their milk. Baiev felt at peace for a moment.

It is compassionate to go and save someone's cow. Baiev had to consider the fact that the time given to the cow would be time away from human patients, but he saves the animal because it is important to the family. I believe that at least partly the reason why he includes this story in his book is that the operation is more significant than simply saving an animal for the sake of the family. Zoyka has a name and Baiev remembers it. He also remembers in detail what Zoyka looked like and what kind of decoration the cow had on her head. Baiev paid attention, took the time to observe, and acknowledged the cow as a subject. The relationship between Umazhova and her cow is intimate, and Baiev recognises the cow's agency. Zoyka provides the milk, she participates in the everyday life of war, and she understands and is cared for. Her body is cared for as she cares for the family. Umazhova talks to Zoyka, and communicates with her through touch, thinking of the cow as her own daughter. The cow, cared for and talked to in this way, allows Baiev to tend to her wound. As Coole and Frost argue (2010: 20), political science cannot ignore bodies and their materiality, thus, "emphasis on corporeality further dislocates agency as the property of a discrete, self-knowing subject […]." The body is an open system in constant communication with its environment. The interaction between Baiev, Umazhova, her children watching the operation under a tree, and the cow Zoyka is a gathering of lived lives in a space of war and peace. Zoyka is real and she embodies compassionate agency as she connects all these lives together. To know war, we need to know about animals too.

Baiev writes about cows at least twenty times in his book. Animals, the mountains, the natural habitat, the whispers of the dark woods are part of the material reality, but also spirituality, which runs through Baiev's writing. It is the understanding of the natural world inherited from the elders. An understanding that the human world and the visible world are not all that is there. Nor is land an object to be only acted upon, moulded and controlled. Such spirituality connects the human being to its environment in a profound way. As war destroys animals and plants, as it burns trees to their deaths and leaves behind abandoned dogs, it attempts to suffocate spirituality, the nurturing force of a happy life. Animals are victims of war too and they are important parts of peoples' lives. Regamey (2014) writes about material violence in the second Chechen war after reading testimonials from human rights reports where inhabitants of Argun said their cows and sheep were living targets for Russian soldiers who shot them for sport. Regamey (2014: 200) argues that attacks against valuables and objects are not only of great importance to civilians' war experiences but "central to the very rationale of violence." Thus, the killing of livestock and looting is not just a by-product of war but has its own rationale.

On the Side of the Wounded

Baiev's book is full of despair, and it describes in detail the horrors of war – literally through the flesh: the suffering of the body and the mind of Baiev himself and all his patients, and those who experienced and still experience war in Chechnya. Yet buried underneath the stories of suffering were stories of compassion and survival. Baiev was asked, for example, by the Russian military hospital to do reconstructive surgery, a proposition to which he agreed. At the hospital, he discussed the number of dead and wounded on both sides with a Russian General. He writes that it felt normal to talk to him, yet strange at the same time because they were supposed to be enemies. "We were both on the side of the wounded," he continues. They even made an agreement with the Russian military hospital to treat each other's wounded. In Baiev's experience, people understood that everyone was a victim of war, and some Chechen families even took war prisoners in as guests, showing hospitality.

Baiev saved and healed ordinary Chechens, Chechen fighters and Russian soldiers alike, and he suffered the consequences. He became the enemy of both Chechen fighters and Russian forces which led to his eventual escape to the United States. He himself was also saved several times. As if by miracle, someone always came and helped spare his life at the very last moment. One time he was stopped and taken into a house by three Russian contract soldiers at a checkpoint on his way to Grozny. Baiev knew that people did not often come out alive from such houses, and if they did, it would be to go to filtration camps to be tortured. The room he was taken to had bullet holes on the walls, blood stains and hair. The men wanted to cover Baiev's eyes and shoot him. But suddenly a Russian major came in shouting angrily. Baiev cried out that he was a doctor treating the wounded. The major said that his wife was a surgeon so out of respect for the profession, Baiev could go, but next time he would be executed. Baiev describes how he felt euphoric and immortal after he again escaped death. Overcoming his fear of death enabled him to continue working and risking his life when so many other doctors, understandably, left Chechnya.

When Baiev worked as one of only a few doctors during the second war in Chechnya, he examined a woman with a leg wound which went untreated because she and her husband could not leave their cellar for a month. Suddenly the woman said to Baiev: "I don't know where my daughter is." She said there were four or five drunk men. "They raped her in front of us," she continued. She talked unemotionally about the rape, as if it was someone else's daughter who was raped. The woman stayed in the hospital bed impassively for a month, and from time to time said, "General Shamanov told his men, do what you like."

Witnessing stories such as this, Baiev became angry at the Russian mercenaries (Kontraktniki), especially the so called Shamanov division. According to Baiev, half of General Shamanov's troops were convicts released from prison to fight in Chechnya. For weeks Baiev could not get the family's experiences out of his mind, and he felt rage when a Russian Kontraktniki was brought to his hospital. He had terrorised people and extracted bribes at a checkpoint. The mercenary had been attacked by Chechen fighters and was hit under his armpit. The man screamed that he did not want to be treated by a bandit. Baiev was tempted to let the man die, thinking, "The world would be a better place without this monster. He would not rape any more women or children." But then he remembered the Hippocratic oath he had taken. "If I started deciding who would live and who would die, where would it end?"

The oath became manifest when Baiev chose to treat all patients, and he did it, in the order of urgency. Baiev's choice to treat all patients regardless of his (conscious) feelings towards them resonates with the compassion of the *Bodhisattva Never Disparaging*, and it represents a political virtue. It is not selective compassion, or compassion which could turn into revenge. It is not discursive compassion: Baiev does not elevate himself as an exceptionally capable and compassionate person. He contemplates right and wrong, resonating with Nussbaum's (2003) vision of educated compassion. In fact, his body does the compassionate work. His conscious emotions are at times explicitly uncompassionate, yet he adheres to and embodies a theistic (Allah) and nontheistic gratitude (his oath). Even when angry and resentful, he treats the mercenaries. Compassion is manifest in his approach to life in general. Returning to the definition of compassion by Brown (2012), rather than a skill set, Baiev's compassion is a spiritual belief about how to live life. It is so profound that he can overcome momentary feelings of anxiety, tiredness, sadness, anger and fear.

Baiev's experiences relate to an ethics of care; an ethics, which as Slote (2007) argues, empathy is essential for. Yet, Baiev's compassion is manifest in his acts, rather than his conscious feelings of empathy, or compassion. He did not feel good about treating the mercenaries, yet he treated them, and not as a rational choice (he risked his life) but because it was the way he wanted to live. Maurice Hamington (2004) argues that embodiment must be recognized as a central factor in moral consideration. For him, "our bodies are built for care;" this is how essential care is in human existence (Hamington 2004: 2). Knowledge on care entails that which the body knows.

I would suggest that Baiev's care is *compassion as a corporeal-political relationship*. Baiev's politics of compassion refuses to take sides when caring for those in need; it is resistance against the dehumanising practices of war. His compassion as an embodied way of life enables him to suppress his feelings of anger and resentment against perpetrators, and to try to save their lives.

Baiev makes a choice – a choice that will manifest throughout the wars. Courage is an interface of compassion in action. To treat looters, torturers and rapists must have been incredibly hard for Baiev. First, he witnessed the parents' pain because of the rape and disappearance of their daughter, and then he needs to treat one of those who took part in the brutal violence against civilians. It is not only that Baiev has taken an oath to treat all patients without discrimination, but he manifests the courage to act accordingly. Even if a moral choice to treat everyone in the order of urgency, perhaps Baiev was also emoting compassion in his body without becoming aware of the feeling itself. The Bodhisattva compassion is, in the end, a body courageously bowing to others, rather than a mind thinking compassionately. Perhaps, then, it was not only Baiev's sense of justice, but his carnal knowledge of the pain of the mercenaries he so despised, which made him the war doctor he was.

In March 1996, Baiev met the Russian doctor Sasha while operating on Salman Raduyev, one of the leading rebel commanders, in a rebel hideout. Sasha was captain in the Russian medical corps. He had been captured by the Chechen rebels for use as a bargaining chip. At the time, Baiev was working in Urus-Martan where civilian casualties were increasing. Baiev needed an extra pair of hands so he asked to place the Russian doctor to work in his hospital. Sasha arrived and started working in the hospital, and Baiev joked that he was their prisoner in the Caucasus, referring to a Pushkin short story. Sasha spent a month there and learned that a Chechen prisoner at a Russian filtration camp for whom he was supposed to be exchanged had been murdered and he would be executed as revenge. Sasha begged Baiev for help, but Baiev did not want to help him, because he would risk his own life. However, Baiev could not get Sasha and the injustice out of his mind. He tried appealing to the field commander, but it was in vain. Eventually, Baiev arranged for Sasha's escape because he could not live with Sasha's death on his conscience. He drove Sasha to a Russian headquarters and before they departed, he asked Sasha to never tell anyone how he escaped. Sasha promised not to, and soon Baiev would pay a heavy price.

Chechen rebels suspected Baiev was involved in Sasha's escape and came to get him at his home three days later. Baiev kept insisting he did not help Sasha but they did not believe him. They took him to the mountains in a Jeep. The men led him to a large opening in the ground and ordered him down to contemplate a confession. Dampness penetrated his bones and darkness surrounded him but he knew he would be shot if he confessed. He felt shame and anger – it was his own people holding him in the pit. Baiev remembers how he had once felt a similar darkness when he was a child returning home from the mountains when it got too dark and he could not find his way. It was pitch dark and he heard a voice calling him. He remembered that the elders had warned not to follow voices into the forest – they were evil spirits luring men to their deaths. He dropped down on his knees to pray and the voice disappeared. He was cold and kept crouched the entire night listening to the sounds of the forest. When the sun rose, Baiev could see he was close to an enormous drop.

Based on how his beard had grown, Baiev suspected he had been in the pit for a week. A guard came to get him up and Baiev felt great pain in his eyes when he saw the light. He knew they would execute him. But first he was ordered back into the pit for his last prayers, and then taken up again. This is when Baiev made his last request for his body to be returned for burial. The rebels started reciting prayers, preparing him for death. But suddenly a car arrived with horn beeping. A man came out from the military vehicle and shouted "Don't kill him! He's not the one!" They drove him back to his village, Alkhan Kala. Without knowing why, he was saved.

Baiev writes that imagining war is impossible if you have never experienced it. But not trying to imagine war means that there is no connection between the one who experienced war and the one who did not. I listened to the story carefully, going to the dark places of my own memories. From this place – him in the pit, me shaken by his story – I was touched by war. The lyrics and melody for the song *Pit* were there. For Baiev, it was, without exception, Allah's wish to save him. In my view, it was the kindness of strangers that saved him. This kindness runs throughout the book and it is, I believe, the essence of compassion. Often there was no explanation for Baiev's rescue. Perhaps his acts of kindness came back to him inexplicably.

Baiev writes,

Chechens believe that to survive not only as an individual but as a people, one must overcome fear. For this reason, I find it hard to write about the war and to admit that after being confined in that dark pit, I couldn't sleep without a nightlight – just like a child. In the dark, I relived the earth closing in on me and my feelings of helplessness. Whenever I heard a noise at night, my heart raced. I broke out into a sweat and had difficulty breathing. I couldn't stay in bed. I'd fling back the covers and go to the kitchen to escape the voices...the voices of my captors.

Baiev is telling this story in the book for the first time, he did not even tell his family before. Sharing the shame and the child-like fear of the dark with the public is a political act. The private experience of fear is the last thing Baiev is *supposed to* admit to, but just as he believes all are victims of war, and all are human, so is he. Baiev exposes his vulnerability, allowing the reader to see him. At the same time, Baiev writes about Chechens as private people who hide their emotions, particularly men, who do not talk about their families. Baiev embraces vulnerability when he decides to publish a book which reveals his personal and family life, his emotions and suffering. He even writes about his depression. The reason for such openness is that he wants to show Chechens as human beings. Moreover, he states that, "The threat of annihilation and use of warfare have conditioned us to hide our emotions lest they weaken us in the eyes of our enemies." What he wants is Chechens to be known, to be heard. War forces people to ignore tradition. In Baiev's case, it means a discovery of an altered masculinity which embraces vulnerability by speaking openly. Were he to be loyal to the tradition which silences, we might not know about the cow Zoyka, his agony over treating Russian mercenaries, his betrayal which saved Sasha's life, or his suffering in the pit and after.

Collective, gendered practices enable and disable social relations and their manifestations. Like Swati Parashar (2011) writes, excessive feeling is often seen as feminine or weak. Writing about war experiences in the first place can mean reliving trauma. For Baiev, writing about his feelings and personal struggles is a step even further. The gendered expectation, as Baiev explains, is for men to not talk about the private and intimate, but to perform their masculine duties without complaint. It is improper for a man to talk about his wife and family, and Baiev apologises for his openness.

War entails militarisation and the favouring of violent solutions (see more in Chapter five). Baiev's compassion is intertwined with militarisation. He accepts blood feud, for example, as the normal practice and means of seeking justice within society. In the war context, though, he does not become militarised. He is not recruited to join Chechen fighters and is able to keep out of the conflict as a result of his profession. What the war seems to do to Baiev, instead of bringing out a militarised masculinity which would seek revenge and take up arms, is to expose his compassion and to feminise him to the extent that he reveals his psychological trauma and its physical symptoms. It is as if the masculine and feminine pressures in him combined to enable both his own agency as a humanistic war doctor as well as his courage to share his story with all its nuances against gendered expectations of patriarchal structures. It is curious that even though war can bring out the worst toxic masculinity, it can also make way for grass-roots resistance to the forces which drive violence. Baiev's stories portray human complexity and political agency which cannot be stilled in stable categorisations.

The way Baiev embodies compassion is through his operating hands and care. When Baiev escaped to the United States after his life in Chechnya had become too risky in 2000, his hands were swollen and blistered from the continuous operations in the warzone, and he wonders if he will ever operate again. In the framework of enactivism there is a living body and lived experience. Baiev writes frequently about the details of his operations but also about his own bodily sensations. He would train physically to keep his mind working. He also did physical exercises in the pit to pass the time. Baiev could not sleep and was exhausted as he had to manage with a couple of hours of sleep, if lucky. He writes, "I worried about my waning ability to feel my patients' suffering, that compassion had been replaced by irritation." When Baiev was staying in Moscow studying skin grafting techniques for a few months in 1998, he began experiencing the symptoms of posttraumatic stress, and he developed a fear of being alone. He did not want to return to Chechnya in such a depressed state as this would upset his family. He describes the psychological and physical symptoms: sadness, heart racing, plunging into darkness, feeling of an electric shock, and sweating. For a moment he wanted to kill himself and even thought about jumping from a window. The next morning he asked to be hospitalised and was admitted for 45 days.

It was not when he received counselling and medication, but when he started exercising again, that he began to feel better. Exercise was the only thing that really helped him during the war, he states. Baiev competed in judo and sambo, which explains his passion for exercise. After suffering from serious posttraumatic stress, Baiev would still experience another war and keep caring with his hands. The body's knowledge of care, the embodiment of care and self-care, is visible in Baiev's war experience, and it attests to the importance of the body for compassion.

Interestingly, Baiev describes how women play an important part in keeping the peace in Chechen society. For example, men must stop fighting if a woman takes off her scarf and throws it between the antagonists. Baiev's autobiography is not only about himself; he writes about many courageous individuals who showed mercy and compassion during the war. Many of those were women, including female nurses who remained in Chechnya to work together with Baiev.

Women in War

> Courageous women. Nurses, risking their lives to save others. They have stayed with him while others have left. And who could blame those who escaped the burning hell of Chechnya.
>
> But the women who stayed to work with Doctor Baiev, the former plastic surgeon
> – now "war zone do it all with no medical supplies doctor,"
>
> these women, when the bomb hits nearby and the walls crumble, they throw themselves against his body...to keep him alive.
>
> Oh they are brave and selfless.
>
> The women use their bodies as a shield. Baiev feels ashamed at the face of such female strength.
> It makes him feel small, even though he is as big as the humanity.
>
> *All this, all this sacrifice is because for them the world is so much bigger than their own lives.*
> *So, they don't have to choose to stay.*
> *The choice is already embodied in them from some moment in the past when they decided, they will never give up.*
>
> (*The Bright place,* Susanna Hast)

In the winter of 2015, I was asked by a colleague, youth researcher Sofia Laine, to perform at a peace event in Helsinki. For the event, I created a two-part piece called *The Dark place/ Bright place*. I will discuss the experience of the performance itself in the concluding chapter, but here I want to discuss the story. It is not simply that I wrote the piece using Baiev's story of nurses shielding him. I spoke the words repeatedly, searched for the rhythm, and did it with passion.

As I kept doing this – working on the text with my body – I began to understand how Baiev's compassion was not an emotion he possessed as his property, but one which emerged in-between bodies; emotions binding bodies together, emotions transmitted and circulating. It was Baiev writing, his experience, but as I thought about the nurses one day after the other, I began taking women in war seriously (Enloe 2004).

Women have been important in the Chechen wars in many ways. Many of the human rights activists and reporters working in Chechnya were women. Natalia Estemirova investigated human rights abuses in Chechnya until she was abducted and killed on July 15, 2009. She worked with Anna Politkovskaya. Eric Bergraut's 2005 film *Coca: the Dove from Chechnya* tells the story of Zainap Gashaeva, who was documenting human rights violations in Chechnya using a video camera. The director explains:

> I have not made a film about high-level politics. Coca was conceived from the start to be about women who struggle against the destruction of bodies and souls; women who condemn violations of human rights and who hope for justice. They don't do this out of naiveté, for which Chechnya would be the place least apt, but because they can and want to do nothing else, because they are courageous, and because they do not deny themselves and their ideals, even if to do so would be easier for them and their families, and would increase their life expectancies (Tribeca Film Festival 2005).

Women also acted as soldiers or took part in terrorist acts, such as the female snipers often referred to as 'White Stockings' (Murphy 2010). Female Chechen suicide bombers, instead, have been called 'Black Widows.' On October 23, 2002, the Dubrovka theatre was attacked by some 40 armed Chechens, 19 of which were female bombers wearing black mourning clothes and explosives on their bodies (Speckhard and Akhmedova 2006a). The macabre images of dead female bombers on the theatre chairs were circulated by the media. Speckhard and Akhmedova (2006a) conclude that the women involved in the terrorist activities did not suffer from personality disorder but from traumatisation, symptoms of Posttraumatic Stress Disorder (PTSD) and dissociative phenomena. They had witnessed violence themselves and lost family members in cleansings and bombings. Many turned to Wahhabism (which was imported into Chechnya around the first war) after their traumatisation, extending traditional Chechen blood revenge to include jihadism.

Speckhard and Akhmedova (2006a: 68) write:

Trauma victims are often dissociative in response to their experiences, displaying amnesia, emotional numbing, and a sense of social alienation. A huge part of the healing process in response to psychological trauma is to reconstruct both a personal narrative and a worldview that incorporates the traumatic event.

Jihadist ideology filled the vacuum and gave women purpose after traumatisation and loss of family members. Speckhard and Akhmedova (2006a) found that the women self-recruited and were willing to join the movement instead of being forced into it. Women are capable of violence, and Speckhard and Akhmedova identify traumatisation, together with religious extremism, as the root causes. Baiev suffered from posttraumatic stress, and most likely the nurses working with him experienced trauma as well. Yet, instead of becoming militarised and radicalised, they cared for the injured.

According to Baiev, on the eve of the first war, throughout Chechnya women of all ages marched through the streets, protesting against the advancement of Russian tanks. He writes that women have always joined the battle, and have even taken up arms when Chechnya has been under attack.   In December of 1994, there was a column of women as long as 40 miles on Moscow-Baku highway. Baiev saw older women make a circle to dance, "their feet picking up the hypnotic beat of zikr," an ancient Sufi ritual praising Allah. *Zikr* is danced everywhere – during weddings and funerals, before the act of blood revenge and when going to war, but its purpose is always to lift the soul to a higher plane. Baiev writes, "During zikr I have heard old men with rusty voices sing like opera singers, and the voices of old women soar with the angels."

Women occupied the streets, protesting during the war and searching for their loved ones after. The journalist Anna-Lena Laurén (2009) writes that only women have the courage to protest on the streets of Grozny. Travelling in Chechnya, Laurén (2009) saw mothers on the streets with photos of their sons who had disappeared, trying to find out what happened to them, to find them.

A woman called Rumani was working with Baiev as a nurse. She transported critically wounded patients through Russian fire. Even if her husband wanted her to join him and their children in Ingushetia, she refused to leave the war zone. Baiev writes (2003: xviii),

> Her courage made me ashamed. She was a woman, and I should have been protecting her instead of asking her to

dodge Russian snipers. Several times during bombing attack, she and another nurse pushed me to the floor or up against the wall, shielding me with their bodies. 'What are you doing' I had asked, embarrassed, the first time it happened. 'We've got to protect you!' Rumani said. 'There are several of us, but you are our only doctor.'

In Baiev's view, he was supposed to be the protector, but instead the two female nurses used their bodies to protect his. This story of the nurses protecting Baiev is only a few lines long, unnoticeable in the grand scheme of war. I became convinced that the role of women was very literally embodied in the way that they kept Baiev unharmed. The women's agency here is not about mothering, escaping, or mourning – their vulnerability has another aspect. They take part in the politics of touch. By touching this way, shielding Baiev, the women challenge gendered roles of the body: the male protector and the female protected. The women risk their lives by staying in Chechnya and utilising their bodily capacities to keep the only doctor they have out of harm's way. They have agency typically associated with masculinity: physical strength and taking control of a situation fearlessly. This could also be seen as a demand for the women to self-sacrifice, but Baiev does not resort to imagery of womanhood or motherhood which would support such an interpretation. Moreover, because women are so easily shamed through patriarchal honour codes, it is important to pay attention to how Baiev attaches shame to himself, not the women. He is ashamed that the nurses have to resort to self-sacrifice for his sake. Again, Baiev's politics of emotions tells a story of embodied compassion and express his own feeling openly, vulnerably. Baiev thinks that war forces people to abandon tradition, especially in relations between men and women, and that it is tradition which holds Chechens together. Yet in the case of his nurses' actions, it is the abandoning of tradition that holds them together, saving lives.

One material need directly related to survival and health in wartime is healthcare. Baiev specialised in dentistry and was a facial surgeon, but had to learn to become a war surgeon who could amputate and operate in the hardest of conditions. He operated even in his dark basement, with little equipment and had a hard time maintaining proper hygiene. The nurses were working under great stress and constant threat. To target hospitals in war, as was done in Chechnya, is a war crime, a punishment against the most vulnerable. So when the nurses protected Baiev, they were manifesting compassion in a very corporeal, even self-sacrificing way. They would rather die than let him die. They were not doing it for Baiev, but for everyone trapped on the battlefield. In fact, Baiev and the nurses were already ready to sacrifice themselves by being in the war zone, facing danger every day. To stay and to care for everyone, without choosing who is worthy of their touch, was their politics of compassion. The nurses were not the only women who stayed to care for the injured. For example, the sisters, Roza and Zarema Asayeva, were voluntary cooks at a hospital in Alkhan Khala, Baiev's home town to which he returned after the Ninth City Hospital was ordered to be closed in 1999 when Grozny was being intensively bombed. Baiev describes how the women took a great risk travelling several miles to work, often through gunfire.

From the emotions, feelings and acts of care by the war doctor, I want to turn the gaze next to a less evident expression of embodied compassion: dance. I return to the role of women in war in Chapter six.

4

Alia

Do you know my story
I think it's unheard of
It's unheard of

I was walking by the street one day,
sunny and warm
When it hit me this thought, maybe I was,
I was immortal

I was passing by the well one day,
cloudy and cold
When I heard the bell calling, calling me now,
calling me beautiful

Do you know my name,
it's Alia
It's written on a stone, I hope

I was walking by the street one day
Sunny and warm
When I heard the bell calling, calling me now,
calling me beautiful

It was a land of the sad
The eternal was agony
The beautiful was long gone
I was hidden deep and
left to the beasts,
to be buried in the ground

Do you know my name,
it's Alia
It's written on a stone, I hope

Faces of the disappeared inhabiting empty rooms, untold names and forgotten numbers coming from the realms beyond touch or reason, the fragmented dreams of a muted presence – traces of the political – imperfectly registered totalities returning to haunt you (Kvedaravicius 2009: 1).

In the prologue to *The Oath*, Baiev (et al. 2003: xvi) writes

During the wars in Chechnya, I knew I could die any moment, so I used to keep a piece of paper in my pocket with my name and address written on it. I always prayed that whoever found my body would take it to my hometown for burial because the Koran commands us to bury the dead within twenty-four hours.

When Baiev is about to be executed after spending several days in a pit, his last wish is to have his body left at the outskirts of his village for someone to find and give him a proper burial. He tells how they made temporary burials for the dead so relatives could a have proper funeral later. They were not only Chechens, but Russian soldiers too. He describes the women of *Mothers of Soldiers*, a Russian NGO, as courageous women who travelled to Chechnya across the frontline to search for their sons, or the remains of their sons with the help of Chechen mothers.

I wondered about the women who disappeared, whose bodies were not found. I had not heard of them yet.

It was Christmastime in 2014. I began to hear a story in my head about someone called Alia. It is still a mystery to me where the name came from. Alia is a product of my imagination, a young woman whose story I invented. Maybe I made her up because I could not find stories told by young women at the time.

For Alia, life is tender and she is happy. But it all changes, the world around her collapses, and she vanishes with it. She is never found and buried.

Alia is my favourite song. It has it all. The funky arrangement celebrates hope and joy while the lyrics entail the tragedy. The song is a desperate cry that also asks the body to move, to dance.

Dance, Synchrony and Compassion

Dance is a physical activity which war affects, and which affects war and political ordering. Dana Mills (2017: 77) writes that dance can witness "those moments that are too complex, contradictory, dense to be expressed in words; those which are in danger of going under the radar; those which defy a singular narrative." The density and complexity of Chechen dance disables a singular narrative because many languages are written on the body and translated by the body.

According to Jaimoukha (2005: 194), dance is the most popular kind of folk art in Chechnya. He writes, "Music and dance are of such potent force in society that they stand to play a central role as rallying cries in national revival and the building of devastated Chechnya once the war is over." Dance, in fact, is the bodily movement that connects collective emotion, national identity, and the private experience. In this chapter, I introduce the idea that dance can imply compassion through kinaesthetic empathy and that dance can also signify perseverance and resistance manifested in the body's movements.

Dance is a multisensory activity. It requires interaction with the social world and physical environment. Dance involves interpretation, creativity, problem solving, sensing of time and perceiving of space, self-regulation, concentration, presence, emotions and imagination (see Anttila 2013). Dance in the context of war is important for understanding how emotions, coping mechanisms, healing and movement are in close relationship. First is the connection to others in movement through flesh, as Damasio (2010) explains, from actual movement we make somatosensory representations and visual representations which become part of our memory. For example, you can remember and recognise someone by the way they walk, or notice how someone's posture reminds you of another person. Even if we do not pay conscious attention to corporeality, we do observe all the time the bodies of others in movement. Judith Lynne Hanna (2015), who has contributed significantly to knowledge on dance and the brain, explains how dance has multiple functions affecting learning and well-being. Dance, is a form of nonverbal language, an effective method of communication which affects the brain in a way similar to language. The physical exercise of dance sparks new brain cells and their connections (neuroplasticity), increases neurotrans-mitters, nerve growth factors, etc. Moreover, dance helps to regulate stress; it has cognitive, emotional and therapeutic functions.

Interaction and movement are central to our brain activity. As Damasio (2010) argues, the brain's mapping of its outside world (the body proper included) takes place in the context of movement. The physicality of compassion is related to synchronised movement. In a clinical study by Valdesolo and DeSteno (2011), when two individuals tapped computer sensors in rhythmic synchrony they reported feeling more similar to each other than towards those with whom they tapped asynchronously. The synchronised tapping also correlated with compassion and willingness to help the other in a task. The researchers then asked questions to determine feelings of liking and compassion, and tested the participant's willingness to assist the person she tapped with. The participant would more likely help the victim if she had tapped a sensor in synchrony with the victim rather than not in synchrony. Valdesolo and DeSteno (2011) refer to this as synchrony-induced compassion.

There are other studies which attest to different affective/emotional impacts of synchrony, such as the study by Lumsden et al. (2014) in which researchers found intentional synchronous interpersonal movement positively affected self-esteem and social connection to the other. They suggest that we may feel better about ourselves when moving in synchrony instead of moving to our own rhythm (Lumsden et al. 2014). To achieve interpersonal synchrony with another person, the individual needs to adjust to and temporally align with, the movement of the other. Cacioppo et al. (2014) found out in their study how the referent person – the one to whose rhythm the other attunes – also experiences affiliative feelings towards the other. They found correlation between synchronised movement and feelings of affiliation in the referent person, thus synchrony affects the emotions of both parties. Launay et al. (2014) found that likability increases even with a virtual partner, and not just by perceived action, but even with only sound. Tarr et al. (2015) have studied how synchronised movement in group dancing promotes social bonding and increases people's pain thresholds. Colombetti (2014) argues that mimicry contributes to social bonding, and that moving in synchrony can help to alleviate unpleasant feelings. Moreover, there is a tendency for automatic body movement synchronisation in interpersonal interaction (Yun et al. 2012). These tests show a connection between synchronous movement and com-passion.

Visible stillness does not mean the absence of movement. There is movement on the inside even if not visible on the outside. The living organism is moving when it is breathing, its organs are living, blood is running through the veins, and so forth. Thus, for example, breath can be synchronous as well, but difficult to notice. Synchronised movements often involve repetition (a sequence of movements and sounds). In comparison, mimicking of other's movement tends to follow behind, because the one following the other cannot fully anticipate what comes next. Tapping a sensor repeatedly is then a much easier means of achieving synchrony than trying to follow someone's body movement – also because sound is involved. It is repetition, the continuation of synchronous movement, which enables synchrony to begin affecting the bodymind.

If we perceive through movement, if we are able to simulate the movement of others, and if synchrony induces our feeling for the other – then compassion is related to movement and dance. Motion is even embedded in the word *emotion.* In light of Damasio's (2010) theory of emotion, movement such as dance seems a plausible part of the politics of compassion. But it has to be emphasised that dance should not be essentialised. There is no essence of dance, or ultimate emotion in it. Dance is not necessarily joyful. Dance can cause feelings of anxiety, fear and shame. There are many dances which do not aim for or spring from joy or happiness. Thus, compassion is not necessarily manifested in dance, nor does it necessarily cause the feeling of compassion. But the corporeal engagement with vulnerability, the self, and the other, contributes to an engagement with emotions, and a possibility for compassion.

In dance theory, the interaction of bodies is sometimes described in terms of kinaesthetic empathy or mimicking. Something corporeal is transmitted from the dancer to the spectator. According to dance professor Susan Foster (2010), this transmission is not spontaneous but born in a historical context of subjectivity and bodily sensations. Thus, both the dancer and the viewer represent a social moment through their bodies. Whereas Damasio writes about the brain's ability to map the body's state, Foster (2010: 2) refers to kinaesthesia, or kinaesthesis, as a "designated way of experiencing physicality and movement that, in turn, summons other bodies into a specific way of feeling towards it." The concept of kinaesthesia, itself, emerged in the 1880s to describe the nerve sensors of muscles and joints which produce knowledge of the body's movement and postures.

The product of dance is manifested in the body. Dance is body language, and often, yet not necessarily, has a story to tell. The experience of physicality and movement takes place in a social moment and is choreographed. Choreography does not only refer to dance as performative art, but broadly to the arrangement of relations between bodies in time and space.

> Choreograph (v.): to arrange relations between bodies in time and space
> Choreography (v.): act of framing relations between bodies; "a way of seeing the world" Choreography (n.): result of any of these actions
> Choreography (n.): a dynamic constellation of any kind, consciously created or not, self-organising or super-imposed
> Choreography (n.): order observed . . . exchange of forces; a process that has an observable or observed embodied order
> Choreograph (v.): to recognize such an order

Choreography (v.): act of interfering with or negotiating such an order (Klien et al. 2008)

Choreography has as much to do with dance as with political ordering. Political agency and community are not pre-existent, but they appear through the body's movement, through choreography (Puumala et al. 2011). Choreography applies to the study of corporeal practices of power and resistance, such as politics around migrant bodies (Väyrynen 2013). Interest in bodily choreography enables the finding of political agency in previously unknown places, outside of pre-exiting categories. Viewing war through the concept of choreography shifts the focus away from abstractions of political and military theory to corporeal agency (Morris and Giersdorf 2016). The notion of choreography is needed in order to establish a relationship between movement and (political) ordering. When bodies move in time and space they arrange relationships, connections, emotions.

Choreography for Foster (2010) is a plan or score according to which movement unfolds, but also an expression of identity. There are always cultural, political and economic values embedded in choreography. Dance implies values, but also memory. I return to what I wrote in Chapter one: a dancer can begin to remember herself (Monni 1995). The dancing body also remembers the political, "the struggle of power over the force to inscribe upon it" and "the struggle itself, the quest for power" (Mills 2017: 75). Dance is then part of political struggle (see Lasarati 2013; Martin 2016; Morris and Giersdorf 2016). Dance is used for political ordering and reordering, for the training of militaries, as a warning for the enemy, and to celebrate victories; but also in resisting power. Dance researcher Rosemary Martin (2016: 208) writes

> Dance does not often feature in current, dominant accounts of the uprisings that have been sweeping the southern Mediterranean region, yet dance has been present in public protests—from the collective Dabkeh 3 being performed through the streets of Homs in defiance of the Assad regime, to dance as an expression alongside theatre, music, and visual art in locations that could be considered hubs of the revolutions, such as Tahrir Square.

Martin (2016: 218) argues, based on her ethnographic research among dancers in Egypt, that "dance has the potential to act as a political utterance during contemporary revolutionary moments." Yet, dance and choreography do not *necessarily* mobilise or function as an organising principle and structuring device. As Morris and Giersdorf (2016) suggest, choreography could also be ontologically disordered. Perhaps dance does not produce a coherent story but contradictions, incomprehension and loss of control. When I first saw Chechen dance, I saw it as embodied compassion, compassion in movement and dialogue. But when I interviewed two Chechen men on dance (Ali and Said 2017), I had to abandon this single narrative because dance was also associated with shame; the shame of enjoyment and pleasure due to religious commitments. At the same time, the interviewed men described dance as bodily protest and manifestation of freedom. I return to this theme at the end of the chapter.

The transformative potential of dance in war is an individual experience, and in this study, it is observed from the outside through aesthetic sensing. It is acknowledged that the dancer can begin to remember herself, the body and the movement which might have been forgotten. Dance is a study into ways of being. Chechen dance denotes spirituality; there is a communal and historical memory inscribed in the dance, but also a personal becoming. Dance in the context of war can be a return to the forgotten pre-war self, or it can be a new becoming. Moreover, it can be a micropolitical resistance of war.

Film Witnessing War

In this chapter, I discuss compassion and dance in Mantas Kvedaravicius's documentary film *Barzakh* (2012) and Nikita Mikhalkov's (2007) motion picture *12*. The films are art that transmit the private experience as part of a wider context of violence and its justifications. They communicate life-states, capacities and emotions, one following the life worlds of Chechens looking for their disappeared family members, and the other painting a story of a young Chechen man's faith in the hands of a Russian jury. Even though they are different genres of film, both are witness to war. *Barzakh* was chosen here because it does not rely on macabre aesthetics. It offers a view of war, not as a spectacle, but through the everyday. Second, *Barzakh* does not portray individuals as passive sufferers, but shows capable people making efforts to live, to find the disappeared, to paint the walls, to dance at weddings. *Barzakh* makes visible the invisible politics: families looking for their sons, and authorities unwilling to help. It shows the emotional side of the economy which produces terrorism for profits, to those taking part in cleansings. It also shows dance in a social moment – the (post-)war – during which people continued experiencing war in their daily lives.

Ilona Hongisto (2015: 11) writes, "What distinguishes the documentary from other cinematic modalities is its involvement with a world that continues beyond the film's frame." As Rens Van Munster and Casper Sylvest (2013) argue, documentary film is not a window to reality but a set of visual constellations of reality. Documentary film is already an interpretation of reality. Hongisto refers to fabulation as one aspect of what documentaries can do. She describes fabulation as the space in-between people who tell stories and the documentary camera that observes these fabulous acts. In that relationship is an undoing of an "antagonistic dichotomy between the true and the false" (Hongisto 2015, 67). Documentaries can then fabulate alternative ways of being in the world. The filmmaker is active, making aesthetic decisions along the way. She shares the moment with the filmed, and chooses the stories to tell, but not the way the viewer sees them.

I am less curious about the intentions of the filmmaker than with the aesthetic as an opening to something not yet conceived or envisioned. The documentaries chosen here are looked at from a fabulating perspective, without the assumption that the filmmaker intended for them to unsettle anything.

Politics is found in the gaps between bodies and in the actions which make the gaps wider or narrower, or which blur the boundary between the private body and the collective body, the self and the other. I return to what I wrote in the introduction: text, film, images and sounds act upon the reader's, viewer's or listener's body. At the same time, the audience is not passively receiving an aesthetic message, but co-creates it from her own experience and perception. Embodied insight is then born *in-between bodies.* Politics does not exist simply between representation and represented as *ideas*, but as living organisms which move in relation to each other. I have developed this idea by moving with a character in the film *12* in order to investigate the possibilities for shrinking the space or negotiating the difference between us.

There are many things to say about politics, cinema and the brain (see Connolly 2002), but I contend here with some notes on film technique and the role of film in politics. Bodies do not have to be in the same physical space to affect each other, as Anthony D'Aloia (2012) explains when discussing cinematic empathy. The film I analyse affects my body (bodymind). The bodies moving on the screen excite my body, activating the brain regions related to movement when perceiving others' movement. D'Aloia (2012) refers to the bodies on the screen as quasi-bodies which present vitality and tension which the spectator can accompany. Moreover, the film itself is a body. Film's "mechanical movements embody human spectator's modes of experiencing the world," for example, in the case of fluid tracking or a close-up (D'Aloia 2012:101). The camera – its perspective, cuts and moves become the body we follow, creating a cinematic embodiment.

The reason I use a fiction film to discuss war experience in the second part of the chapter is that popular culture and politics are not two separate phenomena, they are co-constitutive (Dodds 2015; Shepherd 2013). Popular culture is used in politics (like propaganda) and it is a part of the global economy. Popular culture makes ideas, resistance, ideologies and emotions flow across borders (Weldes and Rowley 2015). While empirical reality is often contrasted with fictional stories of human experience, as Shapiro (2009: 5) argues, "cinema provides superior access to empirical veracity than other forms of managed perception." The film's advantage is the possibility to rewind, to return to the images and sounds, to focus perception on details, and different details each viewing. The film-body can offer unusual and changing perspectives – close-ups, views from far away, above or underneath. There are limitations, because the films perspective is forced upon the viewer, but any kind of observation is biased because the body is not an all-perceiving, all-processing machine. Most importantly, film excites the imagination from a multisensory perspective, leaving smell and touch away, but enabling kinaesthetic, visual and auditory experiences.

Dance Under the Surface

In *Barzakh*, people are living a non-life, waiting for news about their friends and relatives who have disappeared. News which often never comes. The film begins with a misty image of a woman praying for her disappeared son, and is followed by images of water which represents a dreamy state. The film is composed of lingering and longing, stillness and silence, and then – a wedding dance. Dance in *Barzakh* is the politics in-between bodies, a rhythmic rupture in the sensual experience. Dance is not only a great metaphor for compassion, but one possible (but not necessary) way compassion can be experienced. In a group, dancers need to attune to each other's bodies. They are many in body yet together they form *one body*, mindful of timing, synchrony and use of space. Dance is also a great metaphor for and a manifestation of vulnerability. Chechens dancing in the (post-)war context let themselves – their dancing bodies – be seen by others. Dance's aesthetics, in *Barzakh,* emerge as a form of courage, an active and joyful occurrence, even though not everyone present or dancing is necessarily experiencing joy. The dancing body is still vulnerable, but in a different sense: it celebrates life in the face of fear, anxiety, loss and trauma, and the bodily suffering caused by war.

Barzakh was filmed in Chechnya between 2006 and 2009. Mantas Kvedaravicius filmed the documentary along with his anthropological study, and built bonds of trust with his research subjects. He had to consider the risk his work posed to those who housed him, informed him and allowed him to film. *Barzakh* is a film that can be seen as research material, research report, or even a product of artistic research.

As mentioned, during the second Chechen war (1999-2009), Chechnya was established as a Counter-Terrorist Zone which produced terrorism by allowing violence, torture and kidnapping (Kvedaravicius 2012). The normalisation period (still ongoing as I write this), after the active war phase (1999-2000), is presented in the film through glimpses of the reconstructed capital Grozny and the villagers' attempts to rebuild their homes and continue their lives. The documentary is an intimate description of family and village life in a war-torn territory with kidnappings and disappearances casting a shadow on the community. In the film, war manifests through the vulnerable bodies – the scars, the longing and the uncertainty. Wounds are not healing and life is not advancing. *Barzakh* is a state of being between two worlds – past and present – a dreadful living as though waiting for a loved one to return, not knowing if the disappeared is still alive.

The beginning of the film shows a family trying to launch a legal process in order to find out what happened to their missing family member, Hamdan, one of the thousands disappeared. The scene is like a painting, lasting almost 20 seconds. The family members are positioned in groups of two, one pair in the front and the children at the back. Their heads are down and nothing is happening but waiting. In contrast to such stillness and silence, at about 10 minutes, there is a wedding scene – lively and loud. This scene, consisting of dance and music, enters between two silent scenes, as if breaking the dominant war narrative. Through dance, *Barzakh* comes up to the surface of the water and wakes those present from the dream – even if for only an instant.

After the wedding scene, the camera returns to a silent image portraying the back of the woman who is trying to find her disappeared husband. She is looking at a distance, away from the camera, not moving, hands crossed. She is an aesthetic subject to me, the viewer, because I cannot know what she is thinking. I have to use imagination based on her body posture, her stillness, the silence and the space where she stands. The woman is staring ahead, her face invisible to the viewer. Her stillness communicates waiting and the frustration of not receiving answers from authorities. The refusal to help the families of the disappeared find out the truth keeps the bodies still, and time stops because hope and despair are kept alive simultaneously. The body movement of compassion can mean approaching and looking towards the other person. But compassion is also in following, mimicking, and taking someone else's perspective, which does not necessitate physical con-vergence. The woman with her back against the camera has not turned her back on the camera, but rather the camera-body is following her. The spectator is looking in the same direction, positioned in the same direction. The perspective does not necessarily make her distant, but close, allowing the viewer to look *with* her rather than *at* her. Compassion embodied is then a focus of the bodymind *in the same direction*. The scene supports this realisation. There is enough time to start wondering: what is she looking at, what is she seeing, what is she thinking and feeling? It takes time to see someone. Compassion is an engagement with time as well.

The transition to the language of movement and sound is striking: young Chechen men are tapping their bare feet on the ground rhythmically followed by silenced bodies keeping to themselves. The film moves between withdrawn, almost sunken bodies, and open moving bodies. The youth is dancing a traditional Vainakh (Chechen and Ingush) dance, *lezginka*. The bodily energy of the dance marks a change from the aesthetics of the surrounding scenes and a transition from sadness to celebration. Dance represents knowing through moving. A dancing pair must move together – they must see each other, and their bodies communicate intimately even when not touching. The tempo of the music and the way people are in the dance as spectators, tell a story which actively (even if non-consciously) resists war's hurtful effects on the body through kinaesthetic empathy directed at the self and others. The wedding scene provides a landscape of non-violence, a kinaesthesia of dance in the social moment of (post-)war, of mourning and longing. Even if dance does not wipe war away, or erase the hurt, it feels like there is a corporeal becoming taking place, a conversation led by the body. At the same time, the scene shows not only people smiling and clapping hands, but people with the same serious faces and closed positions, as if to serve as a reminder of the war's burden on people.

According to Shapiro, focus on the aesthetic rather than psychological subject emphasises images rather than narrative. He argues that "the post-mimetic aesthetic that cinema animates inter-articulates and mobilizes images to provoke thinking outside of any narrative determination" (Shapiro 2009: 10). *Barzakh* relies heavily on images at the expense of (a single) narrative. The same is true for the film *The 3 Rooms of Melancholia,* which I discuss later, and even the film *12* relies on images for its most powerful parts. But the wedding scene is not only about imagery. It is built upon sound and rhythm. If the other scenes are almost as if still, the wedding dance invites the body's metronome to pulsate with it.

There is a woman shown in the beginning of the wedding scene. Her face is radiating with joy and her smile is childish when she watches the youthful dance. Even if I cannot know what she feels, I can see the smile is spontaneous. A forced smile differs from a spontaneous smile – the difference is visually detectable. This difference exists because different regions of the brain handle forced and spontaneous smiles (Ramachandran and Blakeslee 1998). The face of the woman smiling is not expressing the pains of war but the kind side of life. The smile does not mean she did not experience and witness violence, it means dance and music are having at least a momentary, positive effect on her bodymind; dance and music can be comforting, soothing, energising. They can be all that even when the body is not moving because of the brain's capacity to map the body states of others (Damasio 2010). Shadowed by war, people can still enjoy a special moment as it unfolds.

As the scene proceeds, suddenly there are gunshots in the middle of the festivities. Firing weapons at a wedding is part of life in Chechnya so there is nothing peculiar about it – combat officers are known to carry their AK-47s and shoot them into the air while dancing at weddings (Kvedaravicius 2012). A man in a uniform fired the gun, and he decides to join the dance, leaving the gun aside. The same woman who danced with the talented and fit young men keeps dancing with the officer. The PPSM on his uniform indicates that he belongs to a security force under the Chechen Ministry of Interior. Judging by his uniform, he is part of the so-called Kadyrov regiment, or *kadyrovtsy*, which fights the insurgency under the leadership of President Ramzan Kadyrov, who has been accused of human rights violations such as torture and kidnapping.

People show signs of discomfort in body postures as the officer enters the wedding party. Guests' eyes wander and the film does not show anyone greeting him or initiating contact with him. In Chechnya, homes and parties have open doors even to strangers, yet I do not know if the officer was a wanted guest, except for reading the body language, which indicates he was not. From an aesthetic perspective, the soldier enters and leaves as if intruding peacefully. His entrance and exit, with rifle firing in the air, is shown in the film, when other guests are shown already present, and not leaving. Whoever the man is to those present, he enters with a uniform that does not signal security, but murder, kidnapping, torture and corruption (see Kvedaravicius 2012). The frames of entering and leaving make this a visit of a visibly militarised body with a weapon and a uniform wanting to take part in, and make his mark on, the party. The politics of movement, or choreography, is an officer who is not standing, but dancing; not talking, or staring or taking on any other role but that of a dancer. The dance seems to have attracted the officer to join in an exchange, an interaction, which connects him to others present despite his possible separation from others due to his position, his clothing and his gun.

Returning to what I wrote in earlier chapters on the almost decade long counter-terrorist operation in Chechnya, healing and reconciliation has involved the presence of violence and the complexity of enmities.

Kvedaravicius (2012) explains how terrorists are simultaneously produced and destroyed. People change sides when security and financial interests are at stake. Different agents, groups and institutions are abundant. "Thus, military battalions, combat units and institutions with strange acronyms, and special groups, police stations, prosecutors' offices, and courthouses [...] were now vying and collaborating in the production of terrorists while other, complex, post-war entanglements were weighing upon them" (Kvedaravicius 2012: 14). Kvedaravicius shows that there is no post-war situation in Chechnya because war and peace are not dichotomous.

Dance here is a coming together in the context of (post-)war, and maintaining the traditions, that were at risk of being lost during the war. The choreography of *lezginka* is also cultural. According to Lecha Ilyasov (2009), there are many genres of Chechen folk dances, originating in the milieu in which they appeared, such as ritual dances (like wedding dances), occupational dances (like war and shepherd dances), festive dances and liturgical dances. Chechen dance is marked by solemnity, refined precision of movement, dignity and respect for the female partner (Ilyasov 2009). Traditionally, the female dancer pays attention to the movement of hands and shoulders and the male dancer to the strength of the movement. In pair dance, the partner is not touched. In the demanding version of a male solo, the man beats time with his feet and repeatedly drops to his knees and leaps up (Jaimoukha 2005). Dance is also an opportunity to meet with the opposite sex and perform or show off. Aesthetically, *lezginka* is a very gendered dance. The male and female have their roles to play.

Milana Terloeva (2006) writes that in dance, the woman moves lightly and gracefully while the man is more dynamic and dances as if in combat. For her, Chechen dance is a beautiful, silent, precise conversation. Describing her brother's wedding, she writes that they continued the celebration late into the night, and were happy and joyful as if the war, soldiers, mercenaries, militia members, Wahhabis, and other profiteers did not exist. It is, in fact, the social moment, the not-so-post-war which gives a special meaning to the aesthetics of the scene, proposing dance as political movement. This is where kinaes-thesia and the choreography of compassion meet the social moment. It is where the freedom to move and to dance meets the (post-)war political reality.

Dance can be a means to survive, to move in a difficult terrain and oppressive environment more freely, together with other bodies. An outsider can take part in the dance by simulating the dancer's body state from a distance or by participating in the dance. Many of those affected by war in Chechnya lost bodies that were once nearby. They lost parts of their own bodies and their bodies have been scarred. In dance, something lost can be regained.

Connections can be formed and emotions can be expressed.

Dance in a Social Moment

According to Puumala et al. (2011) political agency means that the body moves and bodies interact in ways that enable resistance. The body is political when it moves towards or away from something or someone – or together with someone or something. In the wedding scene, we can see the bodies moving together, both dancers and spectators. Even as the spectator of a film, you might want to move in the same rhythm. Movement is agency informed or constructed by choreography. Dance expresses identity in cultural, political and social contexts – who a person is, who she was and who she can be. You are the way you move. Dance dislocates the person in war from the category of victim towards the agency of a dancer. I say *towards* because I try to avoid stilling and I cannot know what the subject body actually feels.

When we situate Chechen dance in a social moment, it is not only the war and its continuation but also the socio-cultural context in general that we have to look at. For example, Chechen weddings have their own traditions. One such custom is that the wedding party is mainly for the fiancé's family. Kvedaravicius makes sure we see in the film how the bride does not take part in the festivities and how she seems upset, as if not wanting to marry. The bride's body is tense and withdrawn, and she does not share the same joy as the others. She could be a kidnapped bride (another Chechen tradition, which I address in Chapter six) forced to marry. Or she could simply express what is expected of her. Traditionally in a Chechen wedding, the groom has his own party and the bride's family is at home mourning the loss of their daughter. The bride remains standing and silent at the wedding, which can be exhausting (Murphy 2010). So, in fact, the bride in *Barzakh* is an ordinary sight. This is where tradition and culture strongly affect the reading of emotions from the body. What looks like a sad bride to me, can be that, but she can also be a tired bride, a bride who is expected to look and behave the way she does. The gendered expectations weigh on her body.

The idea of compassion is found in Chechen ethics. According to Ilyasov, *Adamallah* (humanity) is a central category of the Chechen ethical system, and it represents the values of compassion, empathy, charity and nobility. Ilyasov (2009: 80–81) uses the term *active compassion* and refers to equality, protection of the weak and abstinence from cruelty (for example in war, towards the enemy). Baiev's *The Oath* is an example of this (et al. 2003). Yet, general moral principles tell only a partial story of compassion in everyday life. Compassion cannot be separated from patriarchy, which defines the woman's role in the society, and allows the practices of shaming and violence against women, and sexual minorities. I return to this theme in Chapter six. The bride, separated from the guests, disturbs the serenity of the dance scene, and makes me think even more about the gendering of war.

Dance as Embodied Compassion

Dance makes a person vulnerable, exposed. A dancer has to tolerate the stare of the spectators. Yet, vulnerable bodies are not weak, they are capable. To be vulnerable is also to be creative. Vulnerable is a life which can be harmed and ended, but the other side of vulnerability – the other side of war – is the compassionate agency enabled by the willingness to be seen by others. Vulnerability means taking a risk – a risk of change, of failure, of shame. In the war context, this risk is greater and more grave. Dance makes the person visible, because it is always somehow special, standing out from other everyday choreographies. It makes a choreography of kinaesthetic empathy. Filmed, the dance communicates to people outside the community, to the international.

Vulnerability and compassion become more nuanced and more complex when sensed from the dancing Chechen bodies. People might not show their vulnerability explicitly. They might not let others see what they feel and what they think, but their bodies in movement, in dance, do. Chechen folk dance is an important cultural heritage, but I propose it has wider implications. Putting one's own body at risk in dance signifies that side of vulnerability that opens up possibilities for healing. In dance, life's precariousness is experienced, and vulnerability is lived as a part of the war experience, not outside of it. As a tool for peace, dance offers an opportunity to get close to or even to touch a strange body. Dance makes possible a particular politics of compassion transmitted from body to body.

Barzakh produces political reality without a promise of truth and it portrays a new aesthetic world. Perception relies on our senses and emotions. Like Damasio (2010) writes, there is no consciousness without emotions. Emotions are like background music, always present in mental processes. Emotions edit, evaluate and order the images that enter our consciousness. Because compassion is so intimately tied to physicality, we can assume that the dance which brings people to interact together through the body evokes emotions, of which compassion can be one. I came to this conclusion through an embodied sensing of the dance. I allowed my body to move with the dancers'. I joined the dance, connected to the rhythm and clapped my hands in synchrony.

Later, when I witnessed young Chechen women dance and sing with pride and dedication, it became evident that dance cannot be overlooked as a site of embodied compassion. Dance was something to relate to, something universal, something that makes a possible platform for compassion because it excites the body directly.

Synchrony in *12*

In the film *Barzakh*, young men are clapping hands in synchrony. It is not casual clapping, but focused and strong in order to be synchronous. It gives rhythm to the dancers, focuses them, energises their bodies and sharpens their minds. Bodies in synchrony occupy the same space – they hear and feel each other. The synchronous clapping at the wedding has likely affected their emotions and helped them form a muscular bond. If the neuroscientists are right, the participants are feeling better about themselves, and about each other, while clapping.

In the Russian film *12* directed by Nikita Mikhalkov (2007), a young Chechen man is waiting in his solitary cell accused of the murder of his Russian stepfather, a military officer who was a family friend to his parents. The jury, consisting of twelve male members, will decide his fate. They are escorted to a school gym with orders to come out after they have reached a unitary decision. When the door is opened for them, the prison cell door is opened to the young Chechen man, as if at the exact same time.

Because he is Chechen, all of the members except one are ready to vote him guilty. He says to the others that the Chechen man is a human being, so they should at least talk first before condemning him to a life sentence. The others are surprised because they believe it is such an obvious case – of course he is guilty. But regardless of their prejudice, the one man's compassion begins to take root, to spread. The one member of the jury cannot know how the young man in the cell is feeling, or what his life was like. He does not know the man, and has been shown evidence indicating the young Chechen is guilty. But he has compassion towards him as a human being, and it is all that matters.

The accused is sitting with his eyes closed in the cell, and the film shows a destroyed house – the accused's home. The film travels between the spaces of the gym, the cell and Chechnya. The man's story unravels at the same time and is temporally intertwined with the stories of the members of the jury. As the members of the jury let themselves be seen, they, and the film audience, begin to see the Chechen man. The men are all sharing their life stories – their fears, their losses, their love – one after the other. As they open up about their lives, they realise that they have all suffered, and the accused Chechen man in the cell is no exception. Everyone has their story, and pain others know nothing about. Unlike the men of the jury, the young Chechen has no voice to tell his story. He has no personality for the jury. They do not call him by his name. But the camera-body acts as his voice, showing images of his past to the viewers. The jury is unable to see the frames, but they still begin to feel the young man's existence and presence.

The jury votes again to see if anyone has changed their mind. When the chairman reads aloud the second vote "not guilty," an opening of eyes takes place. The eyes of the man who first defended the accused Chechen open wide, and simultaneously, almost as if in synchrony, the accused's eyes also open as he waits in his cell.

While two members of the jury have voted "not guilty," the Chechen man walks back and forth in his small cell with some rays of light from the window reflected on the wall creating spaces of light and shadow. It is cold and the accused wears his winter clothes. He paces in the cell and opens and closes his fists. We travel to his home again, but this time it is not ruined and there is a dog barking outside. There are chickens in their yard and a woman walks by with goats. It is a serene sight. He is a little boy playing with a toy tanker, and the Russian officer is outside on the porch with the boy's parents. We move to a scene with chicken feathers and a bullet on the ground, and then return back to the cell which is empty. The Chechen man is outside the frame, as if he had stopped somewhere to reminisce.

The light in the cell is almost gone as the jury keeps on discussing. The accused gets up sitting, trying to keep warm. Back at the gym it is also getting dark, and yet one man votes "not guilty." A choreography of kinaesthetic empathy begins to unfold between the young man in the cell, and the jury members in the gym – bodies connected through choreography but not their physical presence. Back in the cell, the young Chechen begins moving his arms to get warm. But he is not moving only to warm up. The movement is more meaningful, it makes his body remember. The movement transforms to a dance: the young man's hands move close to his chest, and down at his side in repetition, while he lifts his legs up gently, not yet energetically. At the school gym, one by one the members of the jury begin to challenge their prejudice, and vote "not guilty." A bird suddenly flies wildly around in the gym, captive in the space, but free to fly.

Voting "not guilty" is not a decision based on rational thought. Evidence of the young Chechen's innocence begins to mount only when several members have already changed their minds. To vote "not guilty" seems an emotional decision, and here emotional is not meant as a negative feature. The members of the jury do not change their minds because they would have evidence to support the young man's innocence, but because they begin to reflect on their own lives. They share intimate stories of their own life tragedies, or tragedies of people they knew. They tap into their own suffering, and begin to see that they might have been wrong about the Chechen. They might be all wrong about him. They do not know him, his story or his life. They do not know how he danced with Chechen fighters, how his father commanded him to return home from the bad company, how his parents were killed by these same fighters, how his dog died on the street when the shooting began, or how the Russian officer found him hiding amidst rotting corpses in a cellar.

The film takes the viewer back to the dark prison cell in which the young man has started dancing again, turning in pirouettes and marching. He has a smile on his face, hope in the corner of his eye, and his movement has become bigger, more determined. It is no longer a warm up, it is an expression of not giving up. The dance reflects an internal state rather than external circum-stances. He is imprisoned, but his spirit is free. And when the camera returns to the gym, the image from the prison cell and the voice from the jury overlap as if to underline the coincidental nature of the events in the two spaces.

The bird keeps flying around and the members of the jury begin to approach the truth. The young man in the cell is like the bird in the gym - when he dances he has wings. He cannot escape, but his dance will not be taken away from him. When he dances, the jury realises that the Russian officer, the young man's step-father, Volodya, was killed because he refused to leave his apartment which would be demolished to make way for luxury buildings and profit. One more changes his mind, and the camera goes back to the cell where the accused is making skilful pirouettes, with even more optimism in his body and face.

Only one member of the jury is still voting "guilty." He is the one who knew all along the young man was not guilty, but wanted him in prison rather than on the street where the real killers would find him, or before he would find them. This member of the jury was in war too. He knows Chechnya and Chechen revenge, and he believes the young man would live longer in prison. But he agrees to vote "not guilty," and as the jury reaches that decision, the young man finally becomes a person with a name. He is Umar. Naming is an act of making the individual lives anti-disposable (Enloe 2014b) by recovering who people were, what ideas they had, how they felt and acted.

When Umar is found not guilty, a Chechen dance can truly begin. Umar as a child dancing with the fighters – he is so talented, doing the pirouettes. He is proud with his head up high. Back to the cell, where Umar is dancing; back to his childhood dance; back to the cell. With music now, it is definitely not a warm up any longer. It is hope, vulnerability and connection. Umar is released and he meets a man at an alley, the one who wanted to keep him in prison, the one who knew Chechnya. His name is Nikolai and the actor is the film's director, Nikita Mikhalkov, himself. They talk in Chechen and Umar says his father's name was Ruslan, and that he knows who the killers are. Nikolai promises they will find them.

Umar's lonely dance, so connected to his community and tradition, represents being in a place simultaneously alone and with others. He is in the cell experiencing exclusion, in Chechnya experiencing war, and with the jury experiencing compassion. Physically and socially separated by many boundaries, the jury members and Umar find each other, through synchrony and compassion that is embodied in the personal experiences of the members of the jury and the dance of Umar. The members of the jury do not only tell their experiences but relive them corporeally – they play, act, move, feel sick, sweat, yell. They open up about personal matters and express emotions openly and physically. The men are violent and threatening when they act out imagined scenarios, embodying the violence they are supposedly condemning. At the same time, or rather after their violent outbursts, they become vulnerable as they begin to emote and feel compassion.

There is synchrony in the way that Umar begins to rise, move and dance when the jury begins to see him, and believe in his innocence. It is not only the storyline, but the visuals and the camera cuts – the fast transfers at crucial moments between spaces – that make synchrony part of embodied compassion. There is a spatial element to the choreography between the three locations: the cell, the gymnasium and Chechnya, in which all movement takes place. There is a temporal element to the choreography through memories, and the present circumstances. Remembering something forgotten when bodies begin to move. Synchrony in the film *12* is not synchrony as in the clinical experiments where people felt more friendly or compassionate towards each other because of experiencing synchronous movement with the other. Synchrony is more metaphorical, or even spiritual – spiritual, meaning lives which are deeply and often invisibly connected. Cause and effect seem simultaneous in *12*. The frames of the jury contemplating the value and precariousness of life, and the young Chechen dancing more fiercely, follow in succession. This is the effect of the camera-body: the 12 men's lived experiences merge with the accused's. Their bodyminds change together.

Making a difficult decision, Khassan Baiev decided to treat Russian mercenaries even if he felt anger and resentment towards them (Chapter two). I suggested that he overcame his feelings and did what he thought – and felt – was the right thing to do. According to Jonathan Haidt (2000), moral reasoning is based on intuition rather than careful premeditation. He calls it *social intuition* because reasoning is also affected by what others think. Rational explanation comes after the intuitive conclusion has been drawn. Decisions are often made based on heuristics, such as 'thumb rules' and common sense. But if the decision to be made is complex, a more systematic processing is needed. We do not use complex rational reasoning if we can get by with intuition or gut feeling, which is based on our experiences and interpersonal influences.

Haidt (2000) expresses this with the metaphor of an emotional dog and its rational tail. It is emotion and intuition which drive the one member of the jury to insist the young man deserves better than their hasty decision. This man was once saved by a woman who saw him as a human being when he was at his lowest. Similarly, the other members of the jury change their minds because of the wisdom springing from lived experience, emotion and social intuition. It is social intuition because they are affected by their interaction with each other; that is, emotions circulate between them. This is important because it exemplifies a politics of compassion – a decision-making process in which emotion and lived experience are at the centre. When the members of the jury begin receiving conflicting information contradicting their initial prejudices, when social pressure arises as one after another changes their mind and when their bodies begin to remember what suffering feels like, they finally uncover the empirical evidence of the boy's innocence. It is not compassion based on knowing the accused or interacting with him, it is an overcoming of resentment against a Chechen, an overcoming of arrogance, and a finding of a common humanity. An emotional dog with a rational tail.

Director Mikhalkov is considered President Vladimir Putin's supporter, yet for the spectator, the film comes out as a critique of war, enmities and prejudices. There is nothing glorious about war in *12* and nothing to support Russia's cause. The heroes of the film are the young Chechen man and the compassionate Russian who are ordinary yet extraordinary individuals that resist the hamstringing influence of their environment with their compass-ionate action. Through dance, Umar gradually rises up from passivity to fearlessness, and even if he looks lonely, he is not alone. In dance he is with Chechens, he is with the jury and the jury is with him. He came to Moscow with uncle Volodya, the Russian officer, is recognised as a human being by one member of the jury, and leaves the prison with Nikolai.

Setting the rhythm of the scenes from the jury's room and the prison cell are Umar's childhood war memories – landscapes from the destroyed Chechnya. Dance is related to militarisation in *12*, which Åhäll (2016: 9) describes through the metaphor of dance "because it captures subtle movements, bodies and emotions." But dance is not metaphorical here, it is real. It is dance in a tiny prison cell, a dance which takes shape through tradition and self-awareness. It is a militarised and excited dance which takes place among soldiers and a child who participates, making his pirouettes with a knife in his hand. This knife kills, and Umar is ready for revenge.

Dance as Resistance

When I became curious about Chechen dance, and the relationship between dance and emotions, I envisioned dance as rooted in compassion directed towards the self and others: dance with a partner, the corporeal transmission from the dancer to the spectator, dancing to remember. But I began to think that dance was also a form of resistance in Chechnya. Of course, dance is always an experience of the lived body, and everyone experiences dance uniquely. Nevertheless, dance also has a collective side, especially when it relates to collective identity and shared historical narratives.

Jay Rothman (1997: xi), who helped run a conflict resolution workshop in the Caucasus shares this story:

> One night the vodka was flowing a little more freely than usual, and this 6'5", three-hundred-pound Chechen announced, 'Now I will dance!' The group became still as Shamil began his traditional Chechen dance. Soon he was virtually flying through the air, slapping his huge hands against his knees and feet. The passion of his dance, of his identity, seemed to levitate him off the ground. Six months later when Russian troops stormed into Chechnya expecting a lightning-fast victory, I thought, 'Boris Yeltsin would know there is no way this war will end quickly and easily if he had experienced that Chechen dance.'

Dance in its performative element is a form of resistance. It is resistance through demonstrating bodily capacity, the acquired physical skills and the bodily freedom to move as one pleases. 'Dance like no one is watching' is perhaps a similar affective state – dance without a drop of shame.

I wanted to further explore Chechen dance and its dimensions through two means. First, I asked a Chechen family for an interview specifically on the topic of dance and asked: "When do you dance?" and "What does dance mean to you?" I was able to speak to two men about their relationship to dance. Second, I wanted to explore the kinaesthetics, the sensations of where my body parts are and how they are moving, in relation to the quasi-body of Umar in the film *12*. I made a recording of the chapter above in public spaces, stumbling and staggering, and filmed a dance in which I tried to mimic and mirror Umar's dance, and create my own choreography in relation to his. I mixed the soundscapes and visuals of my recording, the film's sounds, my dance, and Umar's dance into a video.[3]

The purpose of dancing with the film *12* was to step out of the limitations of the linguistic-knowing subject to the embodied-minded subject; that is, to transform text into movement, and to rehearse kinaesthetic empathy. Mimicry, and other forms of bodily encounters, are more direct paths to negotiating difference than verbal communication or any intellectual exercise. Writing this book, I struggled more and more with difference, and how to write about others' experiences, appearances, movements and stories; and I have come to the conclusion that an embodied methodology enables both respect for individuality, and the discovery of common humanity. Kinaesthetic empathy is then an active practice – it can be rehearsed. I did this rehearsal by becoming familiar with Umar's unfamiliar steps, choreography, muscle tensions, spins and rhythms, while being aware of the self and its position. Use of a mirror in the film materialises mirroring as an act of kinaesthetic empathy and the presence of a laptop is a reminder of the researcher's positionality.

When I interviewed Ali and Said in 2017, I found out the two men had a complicated relationship to dance. They see dance as being in conflict with their faith, while it is at the same time an important cultural heritage. They emphasise that they do not enjoy dance and would not dance for pleasure. At first it seems dance is not important at all because when I say 'dance,' they understand it as professional dance, but once we begin talking more explicitly about *lezginka*, dance turns from a profession to an important cultural tradition to be maintained.

Said tells me that Chechen dance is a way of showing off, showing one's skills, and for women, a way to present themselves as suitable wives. He avoids dance because of religious beliefs and repeats the word "haram" or forbidden. Thus, there is a culture of dance, and a religion for which dance does not belong. Said talks about Muslim weddings and arranged marriages, and he touches upon the topic of bride kidnapping, or stealing. He considers bride stealing a good practice because it enables the young to choose their partners themselves. Poor families might not be able to afford the costs of an

---

[3]   https://www.youtube.com/watch?v=iDHfIIlKvD4

arranged marriage, thus bride stealing helps the poor families. Said's view 'unstills' the image of bride kidnapping from a violent practice to a convenient way to avoid the costs of tradition. Said mentions shame related to the practise of bride kidnapping – the shaming of women is the very basis of bride kidnapping – but he emphasises that the kidnapped woman stays in the house with the female members of the family and is not violated against her will.

Dance has several functions other than to become visible to the opposite sex. The men tell me how the dance practices of Chechen girls can help them bond, which is especially important for a diaspora which struggles to maintain its connection to the homeland. Dance also teaches women to behave correctly. Again, dance is strongly gendered, not only aesthetically, but also in how it emphasises the qualities of womanhood and manhood. Yet, they emphasise that *lezginka* expresses equality and "does not repress women."

As a cultural heritage of both Chechen and Ingush (Vainakh), dance is important as such – "you need to remember where you came from," Ali says. He continues, "It is enough to learn the basics of dance, there is no need to become particularly good at it." Dance has a strong affective side to it, coming from movement and sound. The men tell me that dance allows them to show emotions. Ali continues, "Chechen music gives me internal strength." There is thus a personal element of empowerment which comes with music and dance.

We also talk about *zikr*, the Sufi ritual, because it relates to religious practice; but for Ali and Said, who do not practice Sufism, *zikr* is closer to dance than to a religious ritual. *Zikr* is also a fighting dance, a means to attain a state of trance to increase fighting force. The men consider *zikr* a non-Islamic practice even though at least Ali has taken part in it. Ali says he participated in *zikr* because he did not originally understand it is not part of Islam, nor is it mentioned in the Koran. But then he learned more (from the Internet) and understood it is not the correct way to practice Islam. Thus, he formed his own opinion. For the two men, *zikr* relates to the present political order in Chechnya, to Kadyrov's rule. Their criticism of *zikr* as religious practice relates to their critique of Kadyrov.

I ask one more time, what dance means to them, when we talk about the emotional power of dance and music. Ali finally shares this great story with me and explains it later again in an email. In the 1980s, young Chechen men like him were taken to serve in the Soviet army. They took a train from Grozny to Moscow, and danced *lezginka*, the traditional Vainakh dance, at each train station to show their rebellion. The militia could know nothing about it. "This is what Chechens often do," Ali said. They danced to show the Soviet militia that they were independent, that they could not be controlled. Dance means freedom, "being free like a flying eagle," in Ali's words. Milana Terloeva (2006) writes about the dance of an eagle too – the accents of the warrior, the strength the dance gives to the male dancer. It is dance as resistance against the occupier. Chechen soldiers danced this way in wartime, with the aim of upsetting the Russians and showing them their freedom. Thus, dance is no longer something shameful, a bodily pleasure, but it is deeply political, impacting the sensual experience. Dance is a corporeal protest against Russia and a personal tool for feeling stronger.

From dance, I want to take the reader next to the world of children. Children, which are portrayed typically as those in need of rescue; but also children who are not simply victims but personalities who leave their own mark in this world.

5

Fifteen Thousand

I have an angry face all day,
can feel the wrinkles forming on my forehead

I have an angry face all day
I need to testify, testify to your pain

Fifteen thousand roubles for a life unlived
Fifteen thousand roubles for a life unlived
Fifteen thousand roubles for a life unlived
That's how much you're worth

Need to breathe not to freeze
Need to run not to fall
Need to keep moving on

Fifteen thousand roubles for a life unlived
Fifteen thousand roubles for a life unlived
Fifteen thousand roubles for a life unlived
That's how much you're worth

I have an angry face all day,
can feel the wrinkles forming on my forehead

I have an angry face all day
I need to testify, testify to your pain

Fifteen Thousand struck me like lighting, in a similar manner to *Pit*. I was watching the documentary film *Children of Beslan* (2005) after seeing a theatre play on the school attack in Beslan (Hast 2017). A boy wearing a green shirt explains: "Moscow sent us money. They have given me 15, 000 roubles. A footballer came to the hospital and gave each child 15, 000 roubles. An adult who had lost someone got 20, 000." He yawns. "I don't understand how they can measure lives with money."

I saw this young boy telling about financial compensation for the victims. I noticed I was tensing my face. I wondered if I was beginning to show signs of aging because of my anger. But in the middle of the horror story we know as the Beslan hostage crisis, there is a girl who tries to return to the collapsed school to rescue her mother. After three days as a hostage – thirsty, hungry, scared – a little girl would try to get back to the building to rescue her mother. At the same time, the children of Beslan would know how much life is worth in money. Their lives would be deeply militarised.

I made a music video for this song. I tried to reconstruct the idea of a child hiding and running away from danger. I took my six year old to a nearby botanic garden, which would represent 'scary woods.' I chased him with the camera in my hand. It was all very spontaneous and I realised that the Finnish summer night does not really allow darkness to envelop the scenes. Neither is the botanic garden a particularly scary place. But funniest of all was my son who was smiling, laughing and playing. He was not a convincing actor, but I might have had a poor plot too. I filmed, and when I was editing, I thought that I failed to represent the song. But the song is not a representation, and neither is the film. In fact, the filming revealed to me how far our lives at that moment were from those who witnessed the school siege in Beslan. The film was, in fact, a visualisation of that distance, and the safe childhood my son was lucky to have so far.

Children and Emotions

The reason why, in the first part of this chapter, I write about Beslan, which is not located in Chechnya, but in a city close to the border of Ingushetia, is that the school siege was one of the many attacks conducted by Chechen fighters within Russia and was, thus, part of the war. It targeted children, and families with young children who played no role in the wars. The second part of this chapter discusses Pirjo Honkasalo's film *The 3 Rooms of Melancholia* (2004), a film likewise focused on children touched by war. The purpose of this chapter is to locate children at the centre of the war stage to discuss, through aesthetics, their agency, courage, imagination, emotions and vulnerability. Honkasalo's film excites the visual field, while *Children of Beslan* tries to give voice to the children, yet may fail to do so by imposing a narrative through them. Both documentaries show children, not as passive observers or future protagonists, but acting there and then in their daily lives as lived bodies.

Children are seen as particularly vulnerable because of their incapacities, innocence and powerlessness. But as before, I do not adhere to such a conception of vulnerability. I envision courage as inherent in vulnerability. I sought long and hard to find a word to describe what I want to explore about children in war. It is the capacity to act in the world and to touch the lives of others. Sometimes this means simply being present. For example, children give comfort to mourning adults in the film *Barzakh*. They influence their environment by being there. Agency is one way to speak about children in war, and agency does empower, but it can also disempower the individual, putting her in a worse situation than she was in before (Sylvester 2015). Yet, I do not mean to discuss empowerment, not least because the purpose here is not to construct an image of heroic children. Rather, agency here refers to the children's own conceptions of their agency and their survival stories (linguistic and corporeal). The purpose is to show that children are to be seen and heard, and that they have their own stories to tell. The stories told here have been mediated through adults and cameras. I do not know what the children feel, I can only observe them from the outside.

When children witness war, their emotional experiences are a result of the "nature and nurture" that is their biology and their previous experiences together. Every child experiences differently, just like every adult, but it is the developing brain that makes a child's experience differ from an adult's. The younger the child, the less accumulated knowledge, experiences and cultural norms there are to influence the experience, and the less developed are the brain structures that deal with feelings of emotions. I will first offer some remarks based on developmental psychology and trauma-related studies to help situate children's experiences of their agency and embodied emotions.

First, it has to be said that childhood is an ambiguous political concept (Brocklehurst 2006). Adults are considered agents with responsibility whereas the younger the child, the less capable and responsible, and the more innocent, the child is considered to be. Childhood is sometimes represented as feminine with physical and emotional weakness, which Brocklehurst (2006: 12) coins as the "feminization of childhood," referring to Cynthia Enloe's (2014a) term "womenandchildren" – the association of women with children in war. Moreover, representations of children's innocence and vulnerability are produced in the aesthetics of images depicting physical qualities, and again especially feminine qualities. For Brocklehurst (2006) the dichotomy of child and adult is also at the root of the notion of the political, even if childhood studies is slowly beginning to recognise children's agency – their ability to participate in and inform social practices.

Moving beyond the representation of children in war through feminisation, weakness and emotionality, I am interested in a child as someone with a maturing brain and body experiencing and witnessing war in her own right;

not as an extension of the mother's body but a unique and insightful individual who deals with a traumatic or dramatic experience. The difference between the child and the adult is, thus, not constructed upon a feminised, romanticised and depoliticised image of the child. Instead, I argue, children influence their environments, and they shape and change the world around them, corporeally.

An infant's emotional development starts with feelings of pain and pleasure, and by the age of two, children can display the entire spectrum of emotional reactions (Berger 2008). But when we observe children's emotions, we should acknowledge that they are less nuanced, less distinguishable from one another and less controlled than adults'. The way an adult feels and expresses an emotion is not necessarily the way a child does. This makes it hard to interpret what a child is feeling. Moreover, even when a child is given the opportunity to tell something in her own words, the interpretations of an event and related feelings could be already influenced by adults.

Damasio, separating emotion and feeling of emotion, refers to emoting as the non-conscious body process, while the expression of emotion is controllable and educable (2010). Children have less control over their feelings of emotions – the conscious and linguistic – as the brain is maturing. Between the ages of two and six the brain specialises, the cortex matures and memory improves, leading to the development of emotional self-regulation (Berger 2008). Temperament affects the development of emotional self-regulation and so do early childhood experiences and social contacts. Thus, expressing emotions is a learning process, and it is culturally influenced. Emotions are contagious, but especially to a child whose brain is maturing. Emotional control is learned during the play years, as the brain matures and as the child interacts with others. In puberty and early adolescence, emotions are influenced by hormonal changes, and vice versa, while the adolescent brain keeps maturing and emotional regulation further develops.

Hietanen et al. (2016) have been researching the bodily sensations related to emotions in children. The participants in the study coloured on a drawing of the human body, the area in which they felt a certain emotion emerging strongly or quickly. In the second, they could colour the part of the body in which an emotion was felt weakly or slowly. The researchers found distinct distributions of body areas related to specific emotions in different age groups. In comparison to the results on children, adults have more discrete bodily sensations. Interestingly, in this research conducted in Finland, the different age groups from six-year-olds to adults all show activation of the entire body in the case of happiness. Sadness and disgust, on the contrary, differed significantly which suggests that the accuracy with which children can identify emotion-related bodily sensations depends also on the development of emotional categorisation. They also argue that the development of bodily sensation patterns related to emotions parallel the way children begin to use words to express feelings and emotions. This means that awareness of the bodily sensations of emotions shapes the way children perceive and interpret their environments. That is the enactive *mind in body*, a body making sense of the conceptual world. This is the body knowing, the flesh-word connection.

Trauma, mistreatment and stress affect children and their emotional development. Normal development can be hindered and can even result in "trauma-induced developmental pathways" (Coch et al. 2007, xv). PTSD symptoms in children include reliving the event in dreams or play, avoidance of thoughts, feelings, and activities and emotional numbing (Salmon and Bryant 2002). Both adults and children react to trauma physiologically, and are often unable to create a narrative of the traumatic event (Van der Kolk 2014). Their bodies re-experience the emotions of their past experiences, but it can be impossible to articulate the experience. As Bessel Van der Kolk (2014) explains, trauma by nature cuts the individual off from language-based experience, but it does not mean people do not talk about their experiences. Rather than being able to address their inner experiences, traumatised individuals sometimes make up a cover story, which offers some explanation – this is what Welland (2015) describes as performative compassion. To investigate war experience, then, is to be interested also in the pre-discursive, the non-articulable, the corporeal.

War experience affects the child's development in an embodied sense. The behaviour of a child does not clearly reflect her emotional experience, and the extent to which it does is culturally conditioned. Visible reactions can be very much controlled or constrained, and the developmental phase of the particular child, together with social learning, affects the ways in which a child emotes, feels the emotion and how she expresses them. The purpose of this chapter is not to discover the mimetic of children's emotions in war, but to challenge the stilling of the child's experience into an image of a feminised victim. This chapter wants to challenge assumptions about the vulnerability of a child as merely weakness which robs the child of her agency and identity. The following analysis of *Children of Beslan* (2005) proceeds from the question of how children's agency comes forth in a documentary film which lets children narrate and express their experiences of political violence.

School Number One, Beslan

On September 1, 2004, Beslan School Number One, in North-Ossetia, Russia, was attacked by a somewhat disorganised group of about thirty-two

Chechen and Ingush insurgents. It was the traditional *Day of Knowledge* celebrated in the school by the students with their families and relatives. From infants to elderly people, families had gathered to celebrate at the school. But the celebration would change into a siege that would last three days, take many lives and leave scars and traumas for life.

The siege was planned by the Chechen rebel commander Shamil Basayev, who Khassan Baiev operated on in 2000, amputating part of his leg. Baiev would leave Chechnya soon after, hunted by both Russian military and Chechen rebels. Basayev, who died in 2006, had claimed responsibility for not only the attack in Beslan but other attacks such as the Dubrovka theatre hostage crisis in 2002, and the murder of the Chechen president Ahmad Kadyrov in 2004.

Over 1100 people, mostly schoolchildren, were held hostage and the result was the deaths of over 330 people, of which 186 were children (see Scrimin et al. 2006; Moscardino et al. 2007; Ò Tuathail 2009). Hundreds were injured in the siege which ended with the detonation of one of the bombs wired around the gym where people were being held, bringing down the roof and causing a fire. Hunger and heat caused additional suffering for the hostages. The rescue operation was chaotic as the school was being shelled and the building was on fire. Escaping the school in a weak and confused state was difficult (Burleigh 2008). The reasons for the siege are unclear and Ò Tuathail (2009) explains how there were different interpretations among the people in the region. Some accepted the Kremlin's rhetoric blaming international terrorism while others saw the historical ethnic conflicts between Ingush and Ossetians as being behind the attack. Less accepted was the explanation of the Chechen cause, even if Basayev took responsibility for the siege and the group made demands for ending the war in Chechnya.

The BBC/HBO documentary *Children of Beslan* (2005), directed by Ewa Ewart and Leslie Woodhead, was released in 2005. Ewart interviewed some 140 child survivors in Beslan only two months after the siege. The narrators of the documentary are children, with occasional black screens with text discussing the passing of the events. In addition, clips filmed during the siege are shown: videos by the attackers, Russian tanks rolling in, villagers waiting and crying outside the school, and views of the aftermath.

The film begins with a young boy leading the way. "Here, here" he says, and the camera follows. They are in the school, or rather the ruins of it. A new school has been built, which the children attend. The boy guides the crew through the ruins explaining what happened at each location. His name is Alex and he is seven years old. He seems to remember all the details. He is like a documentarist; it is as if it was not him, but someone else who had been a hostage. He explains where they ran and hid with his father, and how one terrorist found them and sent them to the gym with a thousand others, threatening to kill them if they did not obey.

The children in the documentary describe the morning of the festivities at the school, the moment when the terrorists took them hostage, the passing of the three days, the end of the siege and, finally, the aftermath. When one girl begins to tell about the day, the colourful balloons and the cheerful moods of everyone, she has a smile on her face. She could still remember the happy moments.

The children share their survival stories, details of the violence they experienced, the friends and family they lost, the thirst they experienced and the anger afterwards. But the way the children talk is serious. Their faces are serious, and when an older sibling is talking, the younger one sits still and quiet next to her or him. The narration is factual, not only in terms of the spoken language but the body language as well. A girl says she was really scared when she saw the terrorists with pistols. And she tells it very casually, as a matter of fact. Whereas Van der Kolk (2014: 43) argues that all trauma is preverbal, and mentions how children often refuse to, or are unable to, talk about their traumatic experiences, the children in the film do talk and explain with accuracy. Perhaps the children that are unable to, or unwilling to, linguistically express themselves have been left out of the film. The result is the viewer is presented with an image of a narrator-child – a composed and calm victim of violence.

Early in the film, it is shown that what the children witnessed that day is beyond imagination. A boy explains how a terrorist threatened to kill a man unless people kept quiet, and they could not keep quiet, so the terrorist shot the man in the head and he started bleeding from his mouth. Another boy, who looks like he is even younger, stares and has his mouth open while the other boy talks. A little girl, who looks like she might be around six years old, explains how a girl got shot because her mobile phone rang. Her eyes are moist, but she too keeps it together while speaking. Her nose is running and her voice trembles when she says that it's all she remembers.

The attackers installed bombs which hung in the air on wires, and had to hold a foot at the detonator to keep the bombs from exploding. Death loomed above them constantly. Alex remembers the details of where the bombs were hanging. Explaining, pointing with his hands, as he leads the way to the ruins of the gym, in which sun now shines brightly because there is no roof anymore. The basketball hoop is still there as are the wall bars on which children would climb during gym classes.

The children describe how the siege ended: there was an explosion when a detonator was triggered. Then gunfire. Again they have to witness horrific violence. A boy in a green shirt tells how a bullet hit a grenade and one terrorist exploded so that his brain flew into his face. He says it was fatty and slippery; it was horrible. "We were thrown into a pile of bodies," says one boy. People were dying around them, and they tell it as matter of fact. People were melting, one boy describes. He uses his body to describe how people moved on fire, demonstrating squirming. He shows with his own body what living burning bodies looked like. A girl explains how she was looking at children drinking from a fountain; she wanted to run there to drink until a grenade was thrown at the children and they were blown to bits. One girl had found a little cross on the floor and kept it with her. "It helped me survive," she says as she shows the cross she now wears as a necklace.

Survival Stories

Children's agency comes forth in two main ways: their survival stories and their acts of courage. Survival stories (Mollica 2009) and the experience of having escaped (Van der Kolk 2014), are important for healing from a traumatic event. In the very beginning of the film, a girl says she did not believe anyone could save her. She trusted only her own strength, she could rely on herself only. A boy says with a blank face that he knew they would kill them. All he wanted was to see his mother and then die. These stories are not 'stills' of children being carried in the hands of a rescuing adult. They are stories of moving children, children who had and have their own minds, determination, reflections of the event and the choices they could make.

The children were not helpless, even though some might have been hopeless. Some children tell how they tried to save others. A boy tells how he tried to give five roubles to a terrorist to let his mother go. He was trying to buy her mother out. There is a girl who describes how her mom was left behind. She could not find her, and she jumped out of the window. She was lying on the ground with a woman. The woman tried to take her along but she tried to climb back to find her mother. Photo-images are shown, filmed during the siege, where the girl looks skinny and dehydrated. It is hard to imagine with what strength she is moving. She goes back in the gym and another bomb explodes.

Based on the documentary, one coping mechanism for the children was their use of imagination. A boy explains how during the siege, he was hoping Harry Potter would come to rescue him with his invisibility cloak. Another boy was dreaming how a Special Force man or Terminator would arrive and rescue them. The same boy who dreamt of Harry Potter was told by his mother to imagine a water fountain pouring on him. He smiles when he says that, as if going back to a sweet memory.

Everyone in the gym was suffering from physical exhaustion and thirst from being deprived of water for three days. Captive in the gymnasium, they were constrained by the commands of the terrorists. The children explain how they were asked to keep silent and still for three long days. A boy explains that he could live with thirst and hunger but what he wanted most was to talk. It was difficult to keep quiet because he likes to talk so much. They are in a gym which has bombs wired above their heads and it's hot, crowded, and they cannot move or chat. There are pools of blood on the floor. Being unable to move hurts, not being able to touch, or laugh or speak also hurts. Boredom hurts.

The children in the film do not talk very much about their emotions. Thus, in order to learn something about the emotions of the children, I need to focus on the moving of the lived body. One observation is that the children tell about the events without tears. Their factual style of storytelling can be a way of dealing with the trauma (also Hast 2017). Perhaps this is the way they embody trauma. It may look like the children do not feel (consciously), as if they are emotionally distanced or numb, which is a typical PTSD symptom. The older the child in the film, the more verbal they are about their emotions and the ways they deal with trauma. The children are seated when interviewed for the camera; with the exception of Alex who is showing the ruins of the school, they are reserved and do not express much with their bodies. The only visible corporeal-emotional reaction is pausing when talking about something personal or sensitive. The interviewed children could be nervous because of the camera, but even so they are almost unnaturally still. The children had to sit still in the gym too. To my eyes, the children's bodies seated and still are reflections of the physicality of the siege.

The stories become more vivid towards the end when the children are shown in their element, playing or speaking with their bodies. I feel a sense of relief, because the seated children feel wrong. The children, in fact, seem more engaged with their emotions when they are not seated and still(ed). There is likely much more the children experience in their bodyminds than what they are unable to vocalise or demonstrate for the camera, and the sitting takes much bodily expression away from them. There is also a contrast between the children who narrate factually and the adults in tears, shaking and screaming. I cannot help but think how much this contrast is produced by the filmmakers through cuts, the set-up of the interviews and the choice of what interviews were filmed and included in the end.

While it is clear that experiencing a violent siege, and witnessing killing, injury, fear and distress, results in severe trauma and psychological symptoms in both children and adults, as Moscardino et al. (2007) state in their study on caregivers' resilience after the Beslan siege, there can also be cultural and social differences. They write, "In North Ossetia, children are socialized from an early age to restrain their emotional expressions in the presence of adults, to be obedient and respectful, to be sincere, and to be modest" (Moscardino et al. 2007: 1779). Thus, the interviewed children have tried to restrain their emotions in front of the camera. Or maybe they have become serious.

The children tell how the town has changed, how it is in mourning. The children have changed too. A girl in a white shirt says she used to be happy and playful and now she does not want to do anything. The boy who imagined Harry Potter during the siege says they are not the same happy kids anymore. They have become serious and grown-up. Even little boys became adults, he continues. Finally, he concludes that "kids understand everything." Moscardino et al. (2007: 1781) made similar findings when one caregiver reported, "Before they were two very happy boys, but now they have changed radically: S. has become more adult, while A. looks much older. Something inside him has broken." Thus, they found that the caregivers noticed a change in the children towards seriousness and adulthood.

The way children deal with their experiences is associated with imagination and creativity. This creativity is part of their agency. One child recites a poem about the siege, another sings. Another girl draws the terrorists, and then burns the pictures. She explains that by burning the drawing, "I express the anger I feel inside." She says she still cannot show her anger. Burning her drawings is her way of vengeance, and she explains that her need to do harm increases every time she burns a picture.

Children's creativity is a means to structure and express the experience which does not translate into a coherent narrative. To see children's art is to validate their war experiences. Van der Kolk (2014) shares a story of a five-year-old boy who witnessed the planes crashing into the twin towers in New York and managed to escape unharmed. He made a drawing later of the event he witnessed, but had placed a trampoline in the picture, and explained that next time people jumping from the buildings would be safe. He used his imagination to deal with what he had witnessed. He had the advantage of a safe home environment, and he did not experience loss of life in his family. The bodily alarm system which was activated when he witnessed violence was shut down when he was back home because he experienced an escape.

He could thus make sense of what had happened and imagine a creative alternative – the trampoline saving lives – in the drawing he made. In contrast, Van der Kolk (2014) writes, traumatised individuals get stuck, unable to imagine new experiences. The body keeps re-experiencing the danger. What happens in the body is that the production of stress hormones spikes, and it takes longer than usual for the hormones to dissolve. The five-year old boy managed to escape and take an active role in the disaster, that is, he was an agent in his own rescue. As Van der Kolk explains, this sense of agency and managing to escape is critical for the after-effects. The children in Beslan were trapped, but some of the children could experience escape and survival, which might have helped them to heal from the trauma. Moreover, some children explain how they used their imaginations during and after as a coping mechanism. This attests to the self-healing capacities of some children.

Militarisation After the Siege

The children are shown in the classroom of the new school, and they look like normal, happy, healthy kids. They don't *look* traumatised. But it is one thing to look, and another to see. Armed guards are shown, watching over the school. A mother is shown sitting in the classroom watching over her child. Adults are reacting protectively. Children are playing ball happily outside while the guards with guns stand next to them. The armed guards are a sign of the militarisation of the school environment, but so are the children's testimonials. Violent solutions have suddenly become *the everyday*.

The reason why I want to take up militarisation here, in the chapter on children, is that children are at risk of becoming militarised at an early age when they witness war and its aftermath. Children are at risk of becoming militarised everywhere, due to the militarised ideologies and practices of states and societies, and the extensive media coverage of war accessible to children. They become militarised psychologically and physically through daily lived experience. Militarisation means, to quote Enloe, a "step-by-step process by which something becomes *controlled by*, *dependent on*, or *derives its value* from the military as an institution or militaristic criteria" (2000: 291, emphasis in original). In other words, militarisation facilitates the prioritisation of violent solutions to insecurity, and military values and ideas being normalised (Basham 2011). But militarisation does not mean passively absorbing militarised ideologies and ideas. Children make sense of war actively.

Militarisation permeates societies so that children and youth who have experienced war are at risk of becoming militarised. They can begin to see military solutions as heroic and admire that very same militarised masculinity of which they are victims. Like Macmillan (2011) argues, in a broader definition, militarisation not only refers to state policies but to all combatants and non-combatants involved in preparation for war or affected by militarist ideologies. Militarisation is a seductive process which feeds on masculinist values (Enloe: 2000; 2004). Militarised masculinity does not concern soldiers, men, or adults only. It concerns everyone, and becomes a heritage passed on from one generation to the next. In a study on Chechen suicide terrorism, Speckhard and Akhmedova (2006b) found that traumatic experiences and a sense of duty for revenge made individuals more vulnerable to become recruited and self-recruited into radicalism. Both perpetrators and targets of violence can have a similar background of exposure to extreme violence and trauma. This is the breeding ground for cycles of violence which can originate in childhood. Baiev (et al. 2003: 2) explains how war is an ever present legacy in Chechnya, "Even today, mothers rock little boys to sleep with lullabies urging them to be brave warriors." According to Baiev, young Chechen males are trained in fighting skills, and physical strength is encouraged.

The children in the documentary report that the siege has affected their lives and the community. A girl wearing a yellow shirt explains how her neighbourhood used to be lively but now there is hardly anyone there; and the ones who are, wear black clothes and cry. It is important to acknowledge that in Beslan, the impact of the siege – the impact of terror and the military solution to it – affected the entire community. The attack severed communal ties and customs on a large scale. One such effect has been militarisation in the form of idealisation of military solutions. In the film, an older boy, maybe in early teenage years, tells how after the attack he would walk the street with his rifle and check family members' bags for bombs. He builds a model of the school with missiles on the roof. Every house should have missiles, he says.

Children understand militarisation through their lived experiences. They have become familiar with the concept of terrorism through their lived experiences. Whatever they are told and taught about terrorism, they have also lived through the siege, and thus formed their own corporeal relationship to the category of a terrorist. A girl explains she did not know before what terrorists were, but now she knows: they are people who blow things up. The children wonder why they had to suffer this fate. Why were people killed like this? Yet, the interviewed children do not lump all terrorists together. They had encounters with them, and found some kinder than others. One boy tells how a female terrorist tried to offer water and a male terrorist blew her bomb belt up. The female terrorist became a victim too.

Militarisation feeds on masculine values like heroism. Heroism was detected by Moscardino et al. (2007) as an important cultural value in Beslan, affecting local reactions to the siege. For the men of this region in particular, showing vulnerability and emotion is not desirable; thus, the heroic male (adult or child) shows strength. Heroism has a violent side to it too. Many of the interviewed children speak of revenge. Alex shows the room where his father was killed. He walks in firmly, not hesitating, almost excitedly. He shows how his father's body was thrown out of the window. After that, Alex is shown walking quietly, thinking, emoting, as if finally taking the moment to feel. But in the latter part of the film we learn what he is contemplating: revenge. Behind that calmness is anger. Alex wants to go to Chechnya and kill all the terrorists and avenge his father. Alex is not the only one. A girl who lost family and friends says she is angry with the terrorists and could tear them to pieces. A boy is shown boxing – he says he has felt pain and rage and wants revenge. He wants to cut terrorists' throats open. He dreams of being the president of galaxies and fighting terrorists. A sniper would shoot the terrorists down. He does not believe in God, but in Russia and its armed forces.

The children of Beslan have first-hand experiences of brutal violence, terrorism and military force, and they have been shown life's value in money. From those lived experiences they also form conceptual ideas about the world. These conceptions are minded bodily perceptions formed before, during and after the siege. Such experiences change the children and affect their development. As one child says, "We have grown up, we have become serious." Their participation in the world of the political is tangible. The pressing issue is how these children, and their children, grow and will grow into a culture of violence through these experiences, through witnessing war in their own bodies. The children of Beslan are not necessarily militarised because of the siege; rather, the experience of the siege intensifies the militarisation of their lives and creates a turning point in which their interest in and knowledge of organised violence increases dramatically. Thus, seeds of violence are planted deep. The siege is a horrible example of how war spreads and extends, and the daily presence of armed forces guarding the school after the attack is just one example of how war continues to be lived.

The way war continues to be lived is through the traumatised body, as well as the potentially militarised bodymind. In Moscardino et al.'s study (2007: 1779), the psychological reactions reported by the interviewed caregivers of the children included "behavioural problems, including increased irritability, aggression, sleep disorders, lack of appetite, separation anxiety, and regressive behaviours." Many of those interviewed also discussed physical symptoms such as headaches, stomach-aches, and ear pain. One girl in the film tells about her own bodily trauma – being frightened hearing loud noises. Responses to a traumatic event depend not only on individual coping strategies, but also on the socio-cultural context (such as values, and religious beliefs), the caregivers' reactions and explanations, and the availability of therapy or other forms of activity. Parental responses are particularly important for the children's ability to cope (Moscardino et al. 2007). As van de Kolk (2014: 52) explains, children take cues from their parents, and responsive adults can help to prevent serious psychological scars.

When Ewart (2009) interviewed some of the same children five years later, she found the children were still suffering from trauma symptoms such as memory and concentration problems, aggression and behavioural problems, and health problems. Ewart (2009) writes:

> But what struck me most while talking to children today was how their initial fury and hate towards the terrorists have been gradually replaced and directed elsewhere. Many, like Laima, blame the Russian government for not having done enough to prevent the attack and for mishandling the stand-off with the terrorists after they had seized the school. 'If the government had satisfied their demands they might not have blown up the gym,' she said. But with only one terrorist in jail and not a single official found responsible for the attack, some of the children now search for their own answers about what happened and why. Atzamas was ten when, on the last day of the siege, the force of the bomb blast knocked him out. He woke up trapped under a pile of bodies. He says he has tried to understand things from the attackers' point of view. 'They can't be the only ones to blame. I have studied their lives, their school of Islam and I thought hard about the war in Chechnya. If they were attacked by Russian troops, they were fighting to be free. And then they would want revenge on Russia – after all Russia had been killing their children too,' he said.

From the perspective of children's agency and compassion, it is interesting that Ewart (2009) here shows how some children have been trying to understand and find reasons for the violence they experienced. They have become more critical about Russian officials, and perhaps some more understanding towards the Chechen cause. Atzamas' reflection on the violence in Chechnya as an explanation to what they had to go through is an attempt to understand structures of violence, rather than regarding the terrorists as simply evil. The roles of victim and perpetrator become more complex, and there is a possibility that instead of militarisation and dreams of revenge, something different is underway of becoming. One of the children wants to become a doctor and one a president.

The documentary questions the assumption of children in war as merely powerless, feminised, over-emotional, weak and less rational victims. The risk to children's agency after children have witnessed violence is further militarisation; that is, children can begin to prefer and normalise violent solutions. Regardless of the extensive loss and trauma caused to the community and all the affected individuals in Beslan, within the same bodymind which imagines revenge and missiles resides also the capacity to heal. This capacity can be supported by different forms of therapy, familial and communal support. Moscardino et al. (2007) discovered resilience and healing strategies among the affected families, such as the reaffirmation of shared cultural values, affection among children and their parents, laughter and simply being together. These healing strategies are extremely important to study and discuss just as are the causes of violence and the means to end violence.

Children's agency in war raises questions about the brain-body mechanisms after witnessing violence in childhood. It is hard to imagine that the witnessing of violence during the siege would not affect children and adults by causing strong emotions and/or numbness and emotional distancing which reinforces or inhibits the brain-body process of simulating others' body states. The interesting question is, then: How does trauma affect the capacity to emote and feel compassion? Gaensbauer (2011) has reviewed literature on early childhood trauma, and namely re-enactment of a traumatic event in action or play (preverbal). Gaensbauer (2011: 97) suggests that childhood re-enactment of trauma has something to do with the process of mapping one's body state with another's, and the simulation of motor action:

> In its most basic form, reenactment behaviour can be considered as a product of an unmediated 'match to target,' reflecting how the human brain is uniquely programmed, without intentional awareness, to automatically translate the perception of an external event into an internal representation of that event within areas of the brain that organize the motor actions and somatosensory/emotional pathways corresponding to those being perceived.

Thus, what is perceived translates into an internal schema, a simulation, which becomes motor activation. A child learns by mimicking not only behaviour but the embodiment of emotions. That is, learning how with certain movement comes certain emotion, and how with certain emotion comes certain motor activation. Gaensbauer suggests that intergenerational cycles of abuse can be born in this process. Children identify with the maltreating caretaker and re-enact an abusive pattern. The body remembers, and the memories of violence are thus embodied. Militaristic behaviour can become one outlet for living out violent body memories. Gaensbauer further suggests that an abused child does not only internalise the behaviour of the abuser, but the abuser's emotions and motives as well. Some of the children in Beslan dreamt of violent revenge, yet, in the interviews five years later, Ewart (2009) found out some children now tried to understand the motives of the terrorists. Thus, hopefully, rather than re-enacting the violence they witnessed and experienced in childhood, they can also find ways to heal and help others to heal.

Based on the documentary, it is not possible to draw any definitive conclusions about the experiences of the children of Beslan. I have presented merely observations of the object body, and attempted to produce some insight into children's agency visualised in the documentary. The documentary film here is not a representation of reality, and an aesthetic analysis does not aim for the authentic. The film shows a small sample of children, narrating their experiences to the camera only a few months after the siege. It does not allow for evaluation of their traumatisation. Rather, it raises questions about the accessibility of children's insights and experiences, and the ethics of asking children to share their experiences like this for public consumption.

I have been asked how it is that we can say the children really have a voice in the film. The stories these children have heard, the explanations they have been given, the reactions of others they have witnessed, are all a part of their experience as much as their own perceptions and sensations. There is no boundary between the sensual experience of an event, what preceded it, and what follows from it. There is no boundary between the bodies which communicate events to each other. Children have their voices and others' voices simultaneously. You have a private body and you embody the movements of people around you. Agency is not the same as originality, or an existence outside the constrains and conditioning of the environment. While embedded in their surroundings, children make their own conclusions, and structure their experiences.

The film's contribution – or fabulation – is, that it does not feminise children, even though it produces them as "documentarists" of their own experiences by privileging linguistic over corporeal expression.

Melancholia in Images and Sounds

Pirjo Honkasalo secretly took a tiny camera with her to Grozny, the capital of Chechnya, where she shot part of the documentary *The 3 Rooms of Melancholia* (2004). Grozny is shown at its worst, destruction underlined by black and white imagery. At the same time, the film also visualises the everyday struggles in and around war that are linked to different locations and political, economic and social problems. Through three rooms, Honkasalo portrays children in a Russian military academy, children who are taken from their mother from the ruins of the city, and children living in exile in a make-shift orphanage. I am reminded by the metaphor of a puzzle in which images, sounds and mundane details form the story of war, mimicking the fractured and messy nature of war and life. A lot is left open for the viewer to interpret. I analyse the film in two rounds: I watch it, but I also listen to it from the beginning to the end without watching. This way I can focus on the soundscape separately.

The body of the film is a non-narrator, and the film relies on the power of images. It is not only the visuals that are haunting – sounds of footsteps and the sounds of military training at the boy's military academy are equally important. The absence of certain sounds is significant as well. The voices of mothers and fathers are absent. In room number one, Kronstadt in St. Petersburg, Russia at a boy's Cadet Academy on the fortress island, the voices of parents are replaced by military officers.

In the film, the children are asleep and woken up by military commands. The young boys stand in line in military uniforms as their clothes are being inspected. Their lives are deeply militarised – they live in a military institution and are trained intensively. I realise that what I thought was a drill, based on the sound only, is a gym class where boys are running in rhythm: *raz, dva, tri*. Honkasalo introduces some of the children by name and shares what she has learned about them. Kolja is 11 and was living on the street. He writes poems. Misha is ten years old, his grandfather sent him to the Academy. Dmitri is ten years, his mother is an alcoholic and his father is a mercenary and veteran of war in Afghanistan. Popov's parents are alcoholic, he is 11. He was living on the street after his home burnt down and his mother died falling from a balcony. Tolmachev is 12 and his mother is a Tatar fighting in Chechnya in the Russian Military.

Sergei is 14 and from Grozny. His father was Russian and died in the bombing of Grozny. He is discriminated against at the school because he is considered to be Chechen. He says he saw his father's body being dug up from a mass grave. He became lonely and closed-up. Sergei says that the war ruined everything in Grozny. He continues, "I am going to be a soldier. I know what war is. Still, I am not afraid to kill bad people." Sergei's militarisation embodies being both a victim of war and a future soldier. Sergei, based on his behaviour in the film, seems to be a kind young man. He goes to meet his grandmother, asking about her health and if she is cold.

The boys march in the yard, the sound of their feet softened by the snow. They get wild before going to bed. Their faces are filmed with long shots, showing details such as yawning. It seems there is an attempt to keep an intense focus on the children so that the viewer can have a long look and has enough time to contemplate. The information given by Honkasalo is that these children have suffered, but what they are experiencing in their institutionalised military training is left to the viewer to figure out through the images only. The children's faces are still and motionless in some of the close-shots, as if their minds are wandering far away and they are unaware of the camera.

The children do not seem unhappy in their military training. They are so young, and maybe they find safety in a structured and strict way of life, away from abusive parents or the streets. They learn to shoot, and they stare with awe, mouths open, at a close-fight exercise. Yet, the boys still lack the caretaker's bodily touch and care. These boys can experience social physicality through their training, and it is likely that muscular bonding, a corporeally felt sense of being part of a group (see MacNeill 1995) becomes part of their experience of compassion. I wonder how much the filming has affected the way children are treated, and how they behave, because it looks like none of the children have behavioural problems. Like in the film on the children of Beslan, the camera transmits an image of children who are serious, like they had to grow up. Aesthetically, the choreography of children's agency, even inside the military institution, is an active one. 'Things' have happened to the children, yet they are not passive by-standers. They occupy the centre of the stage, they tell through their movements and stillness.

Room number two is called breathing. It is Grozny in black and white with piles of rubble and destroyed buildings forming a devastating sight accompanied by the music of string instruments. Everything looks dead and abandoned. At first, only stray dogs are there looking malnourished. Some people are coming and going from a building which has taken numerous hits and does not look liveable. The military is patrolling the streets. Suddenly, the streets are busy and people are selling vegetables at a market. Others are standing with photographs of their lost loved ones in their hands.

In the ruins of Grozny, I can hear children playing. They play war, shooting. When listened to they sound like ordinary children, but when seen, their environment is not the playground where my children play. Children playing war is a natural and unnatural sight at the same time. What else could they play but war which is around them? They are so excited, except for one small boy who stands looking serious. An older boy takes the small one and begins carrying him while he keeps shooting at the other kids. The small boy has been given a gun too at some point, but he still remains outside of the play. The children are moving and playing – they are active. War's complexity is portrayed in a child's body, simultaneously a victim of war and a beacon of hope – the suffering child who is still and serious, and the playful child who is enjoying what there is to enjoy.

Emoting with Three Girls from Grozny

There is a knock on the door. It is Hadijat knocking. She is the famous 'Angel of Grozny' (Seierstad 2007), the woman who saves children from the ruins of war. Hadijat enters an apartment to take three young girls from their mother to her orphanage in Ingushetia. The mother has worked at oil mills, has fallen ill and is unable to take care of the children. The building is filled with rubble and is partly destroyed. It does not seem like a building someone could live in. The beautiful girls, with their hair cut short, have to leave the mother behind. When Hadijat takes the papers out, the crying begins. At first it is restricted sobbing. The girls are trying to hold back the tears but by the time they have to leave with Hadijat, the crying is loud. These sounds are hard to tolerate.

The scene encapsulates so much of the everyday of war: the break-up of families, the loss of children, siblings, parents and spouses, people becoming combatants, people being kidnapped, killed, abandoned, hurt, removed, displaced. Hadijat's actions – the collecting of children from the ruins – from the aesthetic perspective contributes to the separation of family members. Yet, she enters the process at a phase where others have abandoned the mother and her children, and in which there are no support networks left in the society other than those created and maintained by individuals. She does not remove the children from the mother's care, but from a mother who can no longer care for the children, and the mother is losing the one thing which makes sense when she has lost everything else. The girls are rescued yet everyone is heartbroken.

I will discuss Hadijat's role here because seeing her helps to see into the adult-child relationship which underpins this chapter. It took corporeal engagement, songwriting and two years, to come to these following conclusions. My interpretation was that Hadijat enters the building as an embodiment of compassion. She takes a personal risk trying to rescue children. But when I showed the clip in my class, my students were angry at her because she left the mother behind. They did not assign compassionate agency to Hadijat. I had to return to the film, and then I noticed how Hadijat was in a position of power. She enters the building with papers for the mother to sign as the sick mother lies on the bed with the children beside her. Hadijat has power while the mother and children have none – this is the aesthetics of the scene. While Hadijat embodies agency, the mother is helpless, lying on her bed alone after the children are gone. The children do not want to leave their mother, and of course the mother is in tears too. Some of my students asked why Hadijat could not take the mother with her. That was the tormenting part. That was what made Hadijat look uncaring. Did she really have to take the children? And what happened to the mother? Hadijat looks so determined and calm removing the children from their mother's arms while the mother and children shiver with tears in their eyes, embracing each other. It is a particularly violent scene.

With a more careful look, the viewer is shown how Hadijat takes the children to her lap, wipes off their tears and tries to comfort them. She has tears in her eyes too. Yet, this can remain outside the radar of perception because the scene's dominant sensual experience centres around the suffering of the mother and her children, and the position of power assigned to Hadijat. In fact, the viewer's own compassion towards the mother and the children can prevent the viewer from seeing Hadijat as compassionate. Hadijat's actions in that scene cause so much pain to the children that it can be difficult to envision what it takes from her to do it. Thus, she does not appear to be acting out of compassion. The scene demonstrates the difficulty of determining what constitutes compassion in action. The solution I offer in order to overcome possible bias is an active engagement with emotions through an enhanced awareness of corporeality.

Even if we fail to read the signs of the cultural body (culturally conditioned ways of expressing or suppressing emotions), if we think about the body's capacity to map the body state of another person, the 'as-if' state I explored in Chapter two, sensing corporeally is a means available for the analysis. When the scene begins, Hadijat fills the visual field. It is easy to focus on her body entering the apartment, cautiously but resolutely. It is *her* choreography. A position of power is easily attached to her corporeality. She is in charge. But soon the visual and auditory field receives strong messages from the children and the mother, and their touching interaction, and the focus shifts to feel 'as if' in the children's or mother's bodies. Now Hadijat, the choreographer, has stepped to the side of the stage, while the quasi-bodies to connect kinaesthetically and emotionally with, are the mother and her children.

Feeling strongly with the crying children and mother, leads easily to ignoring the emotions of Hadijat. Perception is selective. Irrelevant stimuli remain out of our consciousness to leave space for the processing of important stimuli. Crying is just such stimuli. Yet the unattended stimuli are also processed by the brain. This is a type of 'blindness;' that is, the eyes see but the mind does not. We feel for that which we attend to, and we might fail to notice an unexpected object in the visual field, or a change in the object or its placement (See Eysenck 2012). The scene can contribute to the stilling of Hadijat as emotionless and cold in her actions because of her position which forces her to restrict her own emotional reactions. The scene aestheticises the mother and children as victims without agency, but at the same time the scene portrays how compassion in war does not manifest in a straightforward manner.

Through the camera we can see from new perspectives and broader angles; we can repeat scenes and focus on different parts and details of the frame. In a real life situation, events happen around us and inside of us quickly, and we have limited capacity to follow everything. I can only speculate here on how the physical and psychological environments of war affect perception and thus compassion. Yet a film analysis enables repeating a scene and forming a relationship with the quasi-bodies on screen and the film-body in order to find the aesthetic insight the film can provide. And what films like *The 3 Rooms of Melancholia* offer to the viewer are the aspects of everyday which escape the news headlines, including the emotional world transmitted through bodily movements, narrations and choreographies. In the case of Hadijat and the aesthetics of the break-up of the family, we can see civilians trapped in poverty and sickness in war, women's role in war, war's effects on families, the need for individual heroes, or family ties, because there is no official agency providing help. We can see many different ways children enact, how they become part of the war machinery, how they find ways to play together, how they want to take care of their parents and siblings. When Chechens say they were abandoned by the world, they have, like these children and their mother, experienced and witnessed that abandonment at a carnal level. The mother with her children has been abandoned by her husband's family after he died in war. "Shame on them," Hadijat murmurs. It is not some abstract abandonment by the international society, it is the everyday losses that Hadijat sees too many of. The children fall asleep in the car taking them to Ingushetia, and Hadijat promises them ice cream.

Seeing Children

Room number three is called remembering. There are sheep on the fields and soft greenness – a contrast to the grey-coloured Grozny. In Ingushetia, four kilometres from the border of Chechnya, the soundscape of war becomes the sounds of nature and animals, of crickets, sheep, cow bells, roosters, horses, water and wind. These are sounds of peace, yet the absence of sounds of war does not mean the absence of war. The sound of a helicopter is a reminder of war. When the helicopter comes close, a little girl begins crying. She stops crying when the helicopter is gone, and she is caressed by an older girl who might be her sister. I try to identify the children, but with their short hair, the girls look so similar. There are several children in Hadijat's care. There are some six boys looking at that same news clip from the attack on the Dubrovka theatre, which the Cadet Academy boys were watching too. Female bombers are dead on the theatre seats. They watch the same news, which portrays the horror of terrorism, applauding the Russian special forces, not mentioning the chemical gas that was pumped into the ventilation system killing many of the hostages. Reading from Rancière (2009), spectators are not passively waiting to be educated. The children watching the news, at the cadet academy and in the orphanage, make sense of war in their own ways.

Pirjo Honkasalo continues providing the names of the children. I hope this does not harm them in the future. Publishing the names and faces of victims of violence is not to be taken lightly. Aslan is 11 years old. He was found in a cardboard box one night, sexually abused by Russian soldiers. Hadijat thinks he is Russian, but he himself identifies as Chechen and Muslim. Adam is 12. His father was murdered in the first Chechen war. His mother could not handle the bombings, became mentally ill and tried to push Adam from a balcony.

There is a very long waking-up scene, these children are not in a hurry like the boys at the Kronstedt Cadet Academy. When the children are so reluctant to open their eyes, there is time for the viewer to reflect. Why does it take so long for them? Are they tired? Are they being woken up too early? Or is it because of their trauma? The scene underlines how little one can know of what children experience. Again, when the boys are caring for the farm animals, I wonder what they are thinking about – Adam in particular. What are the children thinking when they stare into the world so mindfully? As in Kronstedt, trauma seems invisible in Ingushetia; the children do not display behavioural problems in the film.

The film continues with a ritual in which a lamb is slaughtered and its blood is used to draw marks on the foreheads of newcomers. The women, gathered around the sheep with the men, look away as the animal's throat is cut open with a knife. After a long shot of two skinny horses standing in the mist, the villagers are shown attending a *zikr*. Men and boys are going around in a circle chanting like they were hypnotised, living the rhythm and muscular bonding. After a while they stop moving around and start clapping their hands and feet. The women and girls sit and watch. Hadijat's eyes look sad and she sighs. The men go back to running in the circle, and then back to clapping.

We go back to yet another long scene of the children waking up. This time it is the boys, who have an equally hard time getting up. Adam keeps falling back to bed. Did he sleep badly? Did he see nightmares? The boys watch the sky where something, maybe a fighter plane, is flying overhead. There are explosions and Adam swallows continuing to stare at the sky.

The way to find out how war is lived is to look into the everyday rather than be satisfied with generalisations and statistics. The face-shots in *The 3 Rooms of Melancholia* help to show the children, providing an opportunity for the viewing audience to let the mind wonder and begin to notice children's roles and agency in war. But the close-ups also mean that when the face alone is filmed, much of the body and its surroundings are left outside the frame. There is a danger of putting lives at risk by publishing their faces, stories and names. There is likewise some danger of stilling the face into a calm sadness, a melancholia if you like, which is only part of the story. The film shows children in detail, but it does not portray children's coping mechanisms as much as *Children of Beslan* does. At the same time, *Children of Beslan* goes to an even more ethically problematic terrain than *The 3 Rooms of Melancholia* by asking the victims to share their stories, to relive their experiences in front of the camera. Of course, the viewer does not know what happened off-screen in Honkasalo's film or if the children were interviewed or not.

Perhaps coping mechanisms are simply not expressed in *The 3 Rooms of Melancholia* because the children are not interviewed. This makes the children look powerless. But they are not powerless. In the orphanage, the older boys take part in caring for the animals, which can be one way to cope and heal. Moreover, children are shown supporting and caring for each other in all the three rooms. It is one of the many roles children play in war – they comfort and care for each other and the people around them. Care and compassion are not only parts of adults' agency in war, but are parts of children's agency too.

The Three Rooms of Melancholia displays how compassion is manifold and difficult to still. It begs (but does not answer) the question, how does militarisation affect the children, their emotions, their life worlds and their choices in all three rooms? Will the cadet academy offer the boys the safety they need, and will they end up killing in the name of the state? Will they not only gain the skills to take life but the willingness to do so also? How deeply militarised are the lives of the orphans and children rescued from the ruins? How about their compassion: Will they seek revenge for the fate of their parents and their own suffering?

The collective emotion regarding children in both documentaries relates to the loss of innocence and safety and the abandonment and breaking-up of families in war. This abandonment is constitutive of war and politics in the region. While some of the boys in the cadet academy have been abandoned or forcefully separated from their families, they have found a new group to bond with. In the orphanage, the collective loss experienced by the children and adults present also creates an environment which enables communality manifested in collective rituals. Loss and abandonment, hope and the touch of another body, are thus intertwined. It is not only the loss the children experience, but also a discovery of new meanings in their lives.

Hadijat has made herself vulnerable by being shown in this film and sharing her life for the book *The Angel of Grozny* (Seierstad 2007). It is rarely that we think such vulnerability could in fact be equal to compassion. It does not mean she is an angel who never makes mistakes, but that her activism (and that of others alike) needs to be taken seriously as constitutive of politics. The ones who share their stories in the context of war, who refuse to abandon a sense of common humanity, will have enemies because they prove human capacity for resistance and compassion since emotions are shared states that move between bodies. As Swati Parashar (2015: 76) observes, "Angry women challenge gender norms and disrupt the image of the submissive/domicile woman." The women who manifest agency – be it through anger, compassion or both – are inspirations to some and threats to others.

Hadijat's agency eventually mobilised Lithuanian prosecutors and secret service in 2008 to seek the imprisonment of her and her husband on charges which were later overturned after they had served ten months in prison and fled to Finland (OSCE 2010). The Gatayev family received asylum in Finland in 2012. The human rights activist Natalia Estemirova and Russian journalist Anna Politkovskaya, because they embodied compassion, courage and vulnerability are now dead. Perhaps the persistence of women makes powerful men insecure, and perhaps adults begin to look weak if children appear strong and capable. It can thus be easier to ignore the women, and ignore the children, and portray them as people to whom war happens.

War does not just happen to women and children. When news from Beslan travelled to Chechnya, Chechens were shocked and sad. Milana Terloeva (2006) takes the tragedy of Beslan personally because many of the attackers were Chechen. She was studying in France at the time, but her mother tells her how women and children in Grozny went out on the streets with banderols saying: "Let us take their place" (Terloeva 2006).

6

Lonely Night

How can you do anything good,
when you have to worry all the time

I want to marry, want to carry
won't you take this baggage for a while

Joking about, playing around
One more garbage and I'll die

I'm one step away from giving it up,
and then I'll die a lonely guy

It's gonna be lonely, lonely, lonely night
makin' you, makin' you makin' you mine
Lonely, lonely, lonely night

It's gonna be lonely, lonely, lonely night
takin' you, takin' you takin' your time
Lonely, lonely, lonely night

I'm not the same guy who you once knew
I've been to hell and never came back

All I can do is live in the past,
and it's not the life I want for you

It's gonna be lonely, lonely, lonely night
makin' you, makin' you makin' you mine
Lonely, lonely, lonely night

It's gonna be lonely, lonely, lonely night
takin' you, takin' you takin' your time
Lonely, lonely, lonely night

I try to remember how I came up with *Lonely Night*. I have no recollection, but I have a file named "One lonely night" dated 26 November 2014. In fact, I have a collection of songs almost all of which were written within the same period – winter of 2014. Not all of them have been arranged, and most probably never will be.

"Life goes on even surrounded by death," Baiev (2003: 98) writes, telling of the celebration of the birth of his son Islam in the midst of shelling. I kept thinking of how difficult it must be to maintain or form a relationship in a (post-)war zone. How could Chechens fall in love, get married and start families? How could they deal with challenges in relationships, say for example, when someone begins to change because of the war? How could they survive the end of a relationship, or the loss of a loved one? If something seems absent and difficult to catch, or if it lies outside of the frame, this does not mean it is irrelevant. Absence is just the presence of unknowability. As long as there is longing there is love to be found. Love is a fascinating subject not only because it is not the obvious choice for a study on war, but also because it is so common and strange at the same time. Everyone is an expert on love; but for a researcher, love is a difficult concept to work with.

The Word Love

There are many kinds of love, and loving is a way of being and connecting in general, but here I discuss namely the idea of romantic love. My curiosity for love came, first, from the lack of love stories in the research material, and then from their sudden presence. I was lucky to encounter love stories from war time in Milana Terloeva's (2006) autobiography, because such stories are not easy to come across. In this chapter I discuss love through this one young woman's stories. I begin by introducing some perspectives on love from various sources. The purpose of this chapter is to suggest that love can be at the core of war experiences, and that love is a transformative power that leaves a person changed. If love is transformative, it can transform collectively, not only privately. Love, which is transformative collectively, can be a political force.

The conventions and norms related to romantic relationships, intimacy and sexuality are political, and lead to restrictions affecting women and sexual minorities in particular. The political is written on female bodies through shaming, persecution, arranged marriage, and honour killings in Chechnya. I envision a powerful politics of love because love taps so profoundly into our core selves, to the strongest of our emotions, and it manifests in so many ways, from parental affection to romantic surrender.

Helen Fisher (2008) says in her TED talk, *The Brain in Love*, that

> Around the world, people love. They sing for love, they dance
> for love, they compose poems and stories about love. They tell
> myths and legends about love. They pine for love, they live for
> love, they kill for love, and they die for love. As Walt Whitman
> once said, 'O I would stake all for you.' Anthropologists have
> found evidence of romantic love in 170 societies. They've
> never found a society that did not have it.

According to Fisher, people in love show activation of the ancient parts, the
reptilian core, of the brain, below cognitive thinking and below emotions. She
calls romantic love an obsession and an addiction involving risk-taking, an
obscured sense of reality and a craving for more. From the neural
perspective, the same brain regions are activated in both romantic love and
rejection, which is why rejection can be so devastating. Like all emotions, love
is a lived experience. To know about love is to know how individuals
experience love, the art of love beyond the neural correlates of love.

Love comes close to compassion. It is caring for the other, but the
relationship is typically more intimate, more personal and more physical. In
the Tom Stoppard's (1982) play *The Real Thing*, love is defined in carnal
terms:

> Carnal knowledge. It's what lovers trust each other with.
> Knowledge of each other, not of the flesh but through the flesh,
> knowledge of self, the real him, the real her, in extremis, the
> mask slipped from the face. Every other version of oneself is
> on offer to the public. We share our vivacity, grief, sulks, anger,
> joy... we hand it out to anybody who happens to be standing
> around, to friends and family with a momentary sense of
> indecency perhaps, to strangers without hesitation. Our lovers
> share us with the passing trade. But in pairs we insist that we
> give ourselves to each other. What selves? What's left? What
> else is there that hasn't been dealt out like a deck of cards?
> Carnal knowledge. Personal, final, uncompromised. Knowing,
> being known.

Here love is defined as knowing, or rather, knowing through the body. It is
exclusive knowing of another person's body. Yet, I am not satisfied with the
view of intimate sharing of carnal knowledge as all there is to love. Such a
definition emphasises too much our naked selves or sexualised selves, at the
expense of carnal knowledge through compassion, friendship and caring. I

believe that love's essence is not in exclusivity. Romantic love is typically reserved for one person only, but it only means that there is a person to share more with than others. Even the naked self is shown to strangers in certain contexts. Lovers do not share everything. Secrets are kept to the self, or shared with some others.

Brené Brown (2012) explains how researchers even in social work dismiss the study of love because they do not know how to talk about it and how to measure it, even though love is perhaps the most important human experience. None of us would want to live without loving and being loved. In order to start a conversation about love, she developed a definition from the research interview data she collected during her six years of study on vulnerability. Brown's (2010: 26) definition of love goes:

> We cultivate love when we allow our most vulnerable and powerful selves to be deeply seen and known and when we honour the spiritual connection that grows from that offering with trust, respect, kindness and affection.

From the carnal knowledge which sounds possessive and somewhat selfish we move to a definition which includes vulnerability and a spiritual connection. Brown's definition is also broad enough to include more than romantic love. Such love overcomes shame. It means you are not just looked at, but really seen. To put these two definitions together is rather effortless when framed through the bodymind, which is a fusion of emoting and feeling, bodily sensation and conscious thinking, and the carnal and the spiritual. To have a connection with someone means your neural networks are firing affection, and with a bodily experience soon comes a conscious feeling of the affective state. You know you love. Brown is correct in emphasising vulnerability, the willingness to be seen by others, as being able to love and accept being loved. Love is risky; yet so rewarding that it is impossible to imagine a life without it.

Author and activist bell hooks (2001: 6) offers a similar definition of love as "the will to nurture our own and another's spiritual growth." Hooks emphasises self-love, as does Brown. We need to love ourselves first. Alain de Botton (2016) in the novel *The Course of Love* identifies the central challenges underpinning the idea of romantic love: finding the right person, opening one's heart and being accepted. Furthermore, "Love means admiration for qualities in the lover that promise to correct our weaknesses and imbalances; love is a search for completion" (de Botton 2016: 17).

> The most superficially irrational, immature, lamentable, but nonetheless common of all the presumptions of love is that the person to whom we have pledged ourselves is not just the center of our emotional existence but is also, as a result — and yet in a very strange, objectively insane and profoundly unjust way — responsible for everything that happens to us, for good or ill. Therein lies the peculiar and sick privilege of love (de Botton 2016: 90).

To refer to love as if it was a mental illness is somehow endemic to ideas of romantic love. Love is a dependency, a drug, a need. This is an attempt to include the pain of love and love's inevitable end in the definition of love – a destruction of expectations and dreams because there is so much dreaming involved in loving. Pinkola Estés (1992: 140) expresses the drama of love this way,

> A part of every woman and every man resists knowing that in all love relationships Death must have her share. We pretend we can love without our illusions about love dying, pretend we can go on without our superficial expectations dying, pretend we can progress and that our favorite flushes and rushes will never die. But in love, psychically, everything becomes picked apart, everything.

Love dies, passion dies, appetite dies. Yet the wonderful thing about relinquishing is the receiving of something new. A different loving.

Love is also healing. It is both death and life. It is the shattering of illusions and the construction of a new identity, shared to some extent. Love is also companionship and partnership, a gaze into the same direction rather than a stare at one another. Thus, cravings and insanity are part of love, but also a shared path – less exciting but love all the same. As an act of sharing (sharing a house, a bank account, a bed, a life, responsibilities), love is also political. Such forms of sharing belong to the realm of love and politics. What bell hooks (2001: 76) refers to as the "politicization of love," I call *the political potential of love*.

Love and Politics

Penttinen (2013) writes about the romantic relationships formed between Finnish women and German soldiers during the Second World War in Finland. She reasons that it is the intensity of war – the precariousness of life and proximity of death – which enabled love to be nurtured, against all odds.

She has discovered stories of an "unexpected sense of appreciation at finding love" in several memoirs (90). Love is a force to take seriously in war, not necessarily because it is visible on the streets, but perhaps exactly because it is often hidden and secret. Love can help an individual survive war, rebuild a life after war, or love can lead to violence – revenge, for example. In both cases, love has repercussions beyond the private.

Hardt and Negri write in *Multitude* (2004: 351) that,

> People today seem unable to understand love as a political concept, but a concept of love is just what we need to grasp the constituent power of the multitude. The modern concept of love is almost exclusively limited to the bourgeois couple and the claustrophobic confines of the nuclear family. Love has become a strictly private affair. We need a more generous and more unrestrained conception of love.

Encounters and collaborations which bring us joy are love. The love Hardt and Negri refer to extends beyond the confines of the family and the intimate to political projects and the construction of a new society, a new humanity. "Without love, we are nothing" (Hardt and Negri 2004: 352). I believe that romantic love can teach such love, and be a precedent or an extension of loving in multitude.

Yet, love can be dangerous as a political motivator, and can lead to racism, exclusion, and violence. Thus, when Hardt and Negri (2004) idealise the politics of love, they do not mean love which excludes but which includes. The politics of love is indeed difficult terrain – at one end can be a satisfaction of the most beautiful kind, and at the other a cruelty of a crime of passion. Just like the politics of compassion, the political consequences of love can be of a violent and repressive kind, not exclusively healing and connecting. Yet, just like in the case of compassion, the emotion alone is not necessarily a cause of someone's actions. Other variables are at stake. Violence is not the result of love itself, just like violence is not the result of compassion itself. Acts are not reducible to a single emotion, just like the human being is not reducible to the suffering she has encountered.

In her analysis of Hannah Arendt's writings, Shin Chiba (1995) explains that Arendt considers love apolitical, even antipolitical, a force which should remain outside the realm of the public because it tends to exclude the outside world. Arendt (1958) writes in *The Human Condition* that love is extinguished the moment it is displayed in public and that love can only become false or perverted if it is used for political purposes. "Love by reason of its passion, destroys the in-between which relates us to and separates us from others" (Arendt 1958: 242). But it seems for Arendt, for love to become political it needs to be expressed in public, exiting the private sphere. This is a very limited view of the relationship between emotions and politics. Until rather recently, emotions have been regarded as personal and irrational, irrelevant to understanding political issues (Bleiker and Hutchison 2015). Bleiker and Hutchison (2015) write that emotions are seldom seen as positive political forces, even if political events are so often profoundly emotional. The question is not then whether love or compassion are or are not political forces, because both are as long as they are part of the human experience. Emotions will not leave the sphere of politics as long as human beings are in charge of it.

Shine Choi (2013) writes that in South Korean narratives on reconciliation and national reunification with North Korea, love is a prominent theme. She (2013: 120) writes that "they are public narratives of love insofar as these narratives envision intimacy, unity and togetherness as solving complex socio-economic and politico-cultural problems." Choi (2013: 120) continues, "Love, in different variations, is cited as a powerful driving force for propelling the search for solutions to the 'North Korean problem.'" But Choi's conclusion is that such narratives are destructive, making North Korea the other to be eradicated. Such love is oneness which kills the other. Yet, Choi offers an alternative view of a politics of love, through a reading of Hwang Sok-young's novel *Baridaegi*: love as an in-betweenness rather than redemptive love. Such love is "a way of staying open and attached to otherness through queering love" (Choi 2013: 128). This love does not seek a happy union or a lasting embrace, but is aware of love as "between an embrace and standing alone" (Choi 2013: 128).

Lauren Berlant (2011) notes that romantic love is unethical because it involves desire. But is any political concept fully inclusive, fully ethical? I do not think so. I believe the more interesting question than asking if a certain emotion can be the basis of political change, is to look at how it already is. This is essentially an acknowledgement that emotions make politics.

Stories, images and sounds of love, the touch and scent of love, and the many aesthetic displays of love, are moving. They nudge or push one to express, to sing, to dance, to withdraw, to crawl, to escape. The intimacy of love as a driving force cannot be only negative in terms of politics, because that would mean political agents did not love, or did not love when they acted. Love is there, just like any emotion, at the core of political issues. It is no coincidence then that love occupies so much space in the public, and why politics is ultimately passionate. Passionate because we care and are ready to fight for what we feel strongly about.

Violence, both physical and psychological, is present in Chechnya at several levels, not only through the legacy of war. The main element being the idealisation of tradition including the patriarchal structures of power and the acts of shaming. I propose that love could be an emotional basis for practices of political and social change anywhere, but especially in a profoundly patriarchal context. Thus, I envision love as a form of feminized resistance (Motta and Seppälä 2016), not only in war but against the valorisation of violence in a patriarchal order. There is no harmonious society without a harmonious family and community – this is why feminists pay attention to the private sphere, to the micropolitics of intimacy. What Terloeva's (2006) autobiography demonstrates are narratives in which the passionate and loving youth act with love as their concern, rather than idealised patriarchal traditions. Terloeva's writing contrasts Baiev's in this way as Baiev adheres to the patriarchal order. Terloeva does not specifically challenge patriarchal traditions, but she constructs an aesthetics built more on the emotion of love than on rules about how and who to love. When read in the context of the violent practices revolving around honour, Terloeva's stories constitute the aesthetics of a politics of love. Violent practices related to honour undermine spirituality. Thus, I begin by briefly discussing the violent side of Chechen vulnerability and then the politics of love in Terloeva's (2006) *Danser sur les Ruines*.

Women, Family and Tradition in Chechnya

Imagining the shapes and practices of love in Chechnya is quite difficult for an outsider. Such traditions as bride kidnapping and honour killing make it hard to envision what love looks like. "We never use the word love," Khassan Baiev (et al. 2003: 22) announces, "Though that doesn't mean we don't have those feelings. On the contrary, our families and friends are the most precious things in our lives." And he does use the word love on some occasions. Baiev describes that, like many Chechen fathers, his father never showed any affection or paid any compliments. He tells how he got whipped as a punishment for practising judo secretly. "We rarely express our feelings openly," he continues and suggests that it has to do with the strong admiration of resilience that comes from having a history of being under attack. Cuddles would come from female members of the family, and only until about ten years of age.

> We believe love is demonstrated through actions, not words.
> I've always understood love as loyalty and support of family,
> friends; love is education of children, love is helping the

elderly. I always knew Dada loved me – even when he beat me – but the way he expressed it was by preparing us for the difficulties ahead. He did this by forcing us to work hard, endure frequent beatings and numerous lectures on how Chechens should conduct themselves (Baiev 2003: 22–23).

Each family has a different culture of affection and love. For Baiev, family means everything, and so does the idea of Chechen resilience, a survival as a people, which means both communal loyalty and shaming of weakness. Terloeva (2006) similarly expresses the need for Chechens to survive as a people, which has always demanded that Chechens exemplify certain qualities. Vulnerability, as a weakness *or* as the willingness to be seen by others, is not one of those qualities. Not explicitly at least. It is against this background that both Baiev's and Terloeva's openness about their vulnerability begins to signify a politics of love and compassion. In a culture of shaming, embracing vulnerability is a political act.

Marriage is not a personal matter in Chechnya. Marriage is not just two people but a network of relatives; thus, the family one marries into is important. Baiev talks about the kidnapping of his sister Razyat when she was 17. Bride stealing has been tolerated in Chechnya for hundreds of years. By kidnapping a woman, her purity and honour are put at risk. Her reputation is ruined, she might not find a man to marry in the future. The shame of inappropriate sexual behaviour like touching brings shame to the entire clan. After Razyat was kidnapped, elders came to negotiate a resolution and marriage contract. But Baiev's father did not approve of the marriage and sent him to bring her back. After they returned home, Baiev threatened to shoot anyone who tried to come and touch his sister. The kidnapper's brothers came to their door the next day and, even though he felt scared, Baiev greeted them pointing a gun. A neighbour deescalated the situation, and the men left after Baiev fired the gun in the air.

Baiev himself was involved in a bride stealing. It was a situation in which the woman wanted to marry his friend but because of her family's objection, the kidnapping was seen as a solution. It failed and the woman was brought back home and later married another man chosen by her family. It is interesting how bride kidnapping can be utilised by the two who want to marry. In such a case the young couple go against their families, who oppose the marriage, using the bride stealing tradition to their own advantage. They want to marry because of their mutual love. If the woman's honour is at risk, the family might agree to the marriage rather than demand her release. Of course, it is still the woman's honour at stake – her body, her imagined purity – never the man's.

The generation of women of the pre-war Chechnya learned to navigate between the Soviet order which legitimised woman's role in the public sphere, and the Chechen patriarchal order (Szczepanikova 2014). There are working women and educated women in Chechnya (see Laurén 2009), but Murphy (2010) writes that, even so, the highest goal for a Chechen woman is to be a good mother and wife. When the journalist Anna-Lena Laurén (2009) travelled in Chechnya she saw women who did not fit the model set out for them by the society. Social relations are never so simple that people do not escape the stills we try to fix them into. There are certain social hierarchies in place in Chechnya, old traditions and more recent religious influences, yet the lived experience is always unique – never fully controlled by outside forces and never fully independent. Tradition is always changing too.

According to NGO reports, since Ramzan Kadyrov became the president of Chechnya after his father's death, the situation for women has been deteriorating due to the so-called virtue campaign (European Asylum Support Office 2014). Without legal ruling, Kadyrov has been implementing a dress code, including head scarfs, for female students and women working in public institutions (European Asylum Support Office 2014). The president also supports polygamy. Raubisko (2009) argues that Islam is used for political purposes by the regime. Kadyrov's regime promotes the "right kind of Islam" (Sufism but with preference for certain religious practices and symbols) and believers are at risk of being suspected of being a Wahhabi (fundamentalist and potential terrorist) if they show signs of being too devoted (Raubisko 2009: 78). Raubisko suggests that neither Sufism nor Wahhabism is sufficient to explain religion in Chechnya which is entangled with the constantly transforming traditional, pre-Islamic rules and practices of the society. These 'Chechen laws,' or *adats*, emphasise patriarchal authority, kin ties and ideals of dignity and justice. Moreover, two generations of Chechens were not raised with Islam under the Soviet Union, although religion was not totally absent and some Muslims retained certain practices.

Some Words on Honour

Chechen women are seen as the preservers of the family's honour (Murphy 2010). Female honour is intertwined with male honour, or to be more precise, when a woman dishonours herself, she dishonours the entire family – most importantly, its male members. Rape is stigmatised and rarely reported, divorce is rare and divorced women are stigmatised but also lose children to the husband or the husband's family. This is why Chechen women are advised to marry only Chechen men (unlike Chechen men who may marry Russian women) (see European Asylum Support Office 2014; Murphy 2010). And what is worse, women are killed because of honour. There is a haunting story about an honour killing in Åsne Seierstad's *The Angel the Grozny* (2008: 246–51). The story is about Abdul who shot his sister in the back in cold blood because he heard rumours about her. Men kill women because their reputation, or the family's reputation, is at stake. The killer can think he had no choice, it was *her* choice to live a dishonourable life.

Just like compassion could be explained in relation to neural activity (by no means exhaustively, or in isolation of social theory), so could violence and aggression. In fact, taking another person's perspective can also mean adopting violent behaviour through mirroring. Iacoboni (2013) suggests that mirror neurons could be involved also in the contagion of violent behaviour, and could therefore contribute to the mirroring of violent acts in the body. But a feminist reading shifts attention away from pathologising wartime violence. This means, rather than explaining wartime cruelty as a mental illness of the perpetrator, socio-political explanations are stressed. I believe this applies to honour killing as well to some extent.

Enloe (2004), who studied the case of Borislav Herak, who was accused of raping and killing Bosnian Muslim women, argues that systematic wartime rape is fuelled by men's relations to each other. Rather than a mental illness, wartime rape is better explained through masculinity which relies on a soldier/ warrior identity and social bonding among peers. Amanda Marcotte (2016) uses the concept of toxic masculinity to explain gun violence in the United States. She defines it as a specific model of manhood, geared towards dominance and control. It valorises violence as the way to prove one's self to the world and it is associated with a fear of seeming soft or weak. This toxic masculinity coupled with positive reaffirmation from the group affects the brain/body capacity to emote compassion. Thus, militarised and masculinised social cohesion affects soldiering in a way that inhibits compassion, resulting in rape and the mass killing of civilians. Militarised toxic masculinity helps us understand Abdul's readiness and capacity to kill his sister. He is geared towards a belief system in which his own masculinity depends on the honour of his sister, but it does not mean he does not care. Seierstad (2008) pays attention to Abdul's body, describing his fists, his sobbing, his posture, when he talks about the events leading up to his sister's killing (details which I do not wish to repeat here). Maybe this is a sign of Abdul emoting, even if he says he has no regrets. Or maybe it is Seierstad wanting to see signs of emotion, so that the young man would not seem so heartless.

Valentina Rousseva (2004) writes how sexual crimes during the Chechen wars affect women's positions so that instead of compassion they face rejection inside the community in which female virginity and chastity, and male honour, are emphasised. Shame and dishonour take precedence over compassion towards the raped woman. Again, where is the compassion? Where is love? As Brown (2012) says, shame resilience is all about empathy. Empathy makes a hostile environment for shame. Shaming women who are suspected of having been alone with a strange man in the same space is a violent valorisation of toxic masculinity. This is difficult to reconcile with *Adamallah*, the Chechen understanding of humanity I mentioned in Chapter four. Shame is a powerful tool in war. How can Chechens, men and women alike, ever walk through shame in a culture that puts so much emphasis on honour? Baiev's book offers some examples of how patriarchal boundaries are broken down and reaffirmed during war time.

Tradition is a lived experience with many conflicting sides to it too. There is nothing given about tradition. Kvedaravicius (2012: 181) writes,

> But how is one to specify the peculiarities of 'tradition,' 'honour,' 'respect,' 'morality,' 'blood-feud' and '*teip*,' when they turn up unannounced in macabre actualities; in forms, images, actions or riddles. In bits of 'Chechen tradition' voiced loudly by officials each day, in President Kadyrov's orders to women and girls to wear headscarves, while his enforcement agents drive the streets with paintball guns shooting at those without them. Kindergarten age girls go to sleep wearing scarves for the fear of disappointing or upsetting the President, whilst teenagers burn holes in their scarves swearing not to wear them unless their heads are burnt as well.

There are no statistics available on honour killings because the practise remains a taboo, and killers are often not prosecuted (European Asylum Support Office 2014). Murphy (2010) reports several cases of honour killings. The European Asylum Support Office report from 2014 presents several cases of recent honour killings from information gathered from different sources. The same applies to intimate partner violence: cases are rarely reported and prosecuted, and if they are the men are rarely convicted or are punished mildly. Furthermore, there are no shelters for victims of violence (European Asylum Support Office 2014). Another taboo involves sexual minorities, as LGBT rights are practically non-existent in the society. In March 2017, the Russian journal Novaya Gazeta released news about an anti-gay campaign in Chechnya stating that over 100 men have been detained and accused of homosexuality and three have been killed. The response from the Chechen authorities was to claim that there was no such campaign because there are no gay people in Chechnya, and if there were, their families would implement the punishment, not law enforcement (Walker 2017).

Against this background – the burden on the female body – Milana Terloeva writes about love. In these narratives, love is central in the war experience; moreover, several of these stories unstill the lovers from patriarchal structures and honour codes and bring them closer to spiritual and vulnerable loving.

Her Friends in Love

I had not planned to write about love in war, I was supposed to stick strictly with compassion. The beauty of looking open-mindedly at your empirical material is that you can become surprised by what you find. It was this question that began to haunt me: How could people love and be loved in war? What I needed was to come across Milana Terloeva's (2006) autobiography *Danser sur les Ruines: Une Jeunesse Tchétchène* to begin exploring these questions. I focus less here on the embodiment of emotions than in other chapters, and more on the storytelling through which a politics of love is emerging.

In no other material did romantic love come forward so prominently. Love is at the heart of the matter – any matter – including war, exactly because it is invisible until we become curious about it and acknowledge its importance. Love is so easy to ignore. It is often thought of as feminine, and even silly. But investigating love in politics and war offers new perspectives on resistance, healing, and human needs and actions. But studying love in politics requires overcoming our fixation on rationalist modes and models. Again, I must return to the arguments I presented earlier in the book about the disembodied mind: emotion and cognition are not separate. Feeling and knowing are one and the same. There is not a rational self separated from the body and its emotions.

Love also persists in those places where humanity has failed. Love can be found in the hardest of conditions, the driest of land, and the most destroyed environments. Love is central to the emotional landscape amidst war: broken relationships, relationships that will never be, and the loss of loved ones. Love in the world of Milana Terloeva is equal, gentle, and passionate. For her, loneliness, or solitude, is the most horrible thing about war. Such loneliness means feeling alone even when surrounded by other people.

Milana Terloeva (also known as Milana Bakhaeva) is a journalist born in 1979 in Orekhovo, Chechnya. During the first war she hid with her family in a cellar, and took refuge in destroyed Grozny. At the beginning of the second war, she and her family escaped to Ingushetia. After the war, she risked her life studying French at the University of Grozny (now Chechen State University) while anti-terrorist purges were taking place. She was able to study in France thanks to the non-profit organisation Études Sans Frontières, and she graduated with a master's degree in journalism from the Institut d'Études Politiques de Paris in 2006.

In Terlova's autobiography about her life and the lives of her friends, love is constantly present. It is love for life, love for education, love for family, and so often, romantic love and emotional intimacy with a partner. The young women's war experiences stand out in their youthful spirit and in the importance love plays in daily life among the ruins.

War affects the young through their experiences of love. Young women lose their loved ones when they become combatants or manufactured terrorists, or victims of indiscriminate bombings or senseless killings. So often, love relates to loss. Terloeva writes about Kazbek, a university student who was killed in 2001 by Russian soldiers who set the car he and his friends were driving on fire. Kazbek had planned to propose to Madina, a girl who he had picked flowers for and invited for coffee that same day. Their love was cut short by war.

It is not only death which causes loss, but the possibilities for loving are lost too. In *Barzakh*, the disappearance of a loved one causes a painful absence – not knowing what happened (see Chapter four). War results also in the loss of the relationship that once was, or could have been, for the young who are waiting to experience love and family life. The capacity to love can be harmed and destroyed. The person changes, and is unable to love or live 'honourably' any longer. The possibility is lost before love gets a proper chance.

In Grozny, in 1995, Terloeva's friend Ceda is upset and locked in her room because of a letter she received from Ali. Ali was her loved one since childhood. Terloeva writes that they were a perfect couple. But in the beginning of the war Ali's brother was killed and, due to the loss, his father died soon after. This made Ali suffer greatly, and it changed him. The man Ceda fell in love with had turned into someone filled with hatred. Ceda did not recognise Ali anymore, he was so obsessed with revenge. The last time they met Ali no longer had even hate in his eyes, only emptiness.

Ali had written a letter to Ceda. In the letter he thanks Ceda for every moment together, for every look, for every dream. But Ali does not want to share his life with Ceda, because he has turned so resentful.

> Above all, I would like to thank you for every minute spent in your company, for every look, every wish and every dream. We will never get married. You deserve more happiness than that. I will not convict you to live with me, with the person that I

have become, empty, full of hatreds and resentments. I love
you too much for that...(Terloeva 2006).

Ali believes Ceda deserves something better for her life than being with a
man whose only wish is to kill. Ali writes in the letter how his hate controls
him. Ali believes he lacks compassion and honour, which resulted in him
killing an unarmed Russian prisoner. He shot him when he cried for mercy.
"Our treatment of war prisoners with dignity is what you admired Ceda," he
writes. Ali explains in the letter to Ceda that he could not live with his deed,
and had to go live in the mountains, to go to war. But his reasons were not
noble like the others', he writes. He only wanted to kill or to be killed. Ali's
letter ends with the words, "My life will be short, but because of you I can say
I have lived." Ceda dies in 1996, but Terloeva does not want to write about
her death.

Ali and Ceda could not find each other anymore, after war had taken so
much. There is a spiritual loss, loss of connection, and a destructive affective
environment, a breeding ground for hate, resentment and anger. Yet Ali's
letter is a love letter. It is a letter of love as sacrifice. Ali feels he has become
a dishonourable man too angry to live any other life than war. But he
expresses vividly his emotions for Ceda. Again, there is an openness about
emotions present in the aesthetics of the letter. Terloeva does not write about
this as an atypical anomaly, nor does she portray an image of young Chechen
men as incapable of expressing their feelings. On the contrary: love is talked
about not only among women, but among men too. Moreover, love is not a
footnote in war; it is a central theme. Love hurts and love heals. Unfortunately, neither Ali nor Ceda find a happy ending to their love story.

The importance of love becomes evident through the recurrent stories of
relationships. These relationships, formed and broken, are an important part
of young women's and men's war experiences. Ali's letter offers a glimpse
into the feelings of a suffering young man, a voice rarely heard because it is
considered feminine. A life of honour, trauma, escape, murder and revenge;
then, the most tender affection, gratitude, admiration and consideration for a
woman. Ali's experience is a mixture of being aware of how the experiences
of violence have eaten away hopes of normalcy – a complete lack of hope
indeed – and the wish to protect this young woman, a very vibrant form of
love. What we do not find out is how Ali emotes corporeally. He has gained
the capacity and willingness to kill, but other than that there is no knowledge
of his embodied emotions. But it seems Ali is very much aware of his
emotions; he can describe them and he explains his choices through them.
Emotions are indeed constitutive of war and politics, as Åhäll and Gregory
(2015) write. The loss of his brother and father caused Ali to not only abandon

love, but to become a combatant. Ali cannot be stilled to either militarised masculinity or vulnerability. In the face of love, he expresses both. Milana Terloeva takes part in the politics of love by transmitting the story and the affects embedded in it to the reader. Loving is knowing.

Networks of compassion and extended families literally save Chechen refugees who rely on the kindness of their relatives or compassionate strangers. Terloeva, her mother and her brother were hosted by a Chechen family in Ingushetia after they left Chechnya in 1999. There were already plenty of refugees in the house, but after their arrival, yet another family arrived looking for shelter. The owner of the house refused them because the house was too full already. The owner's daughter begged her mother to take them in, throwing herself at her mother's feet, offering her own place in the house for the family on the street. Her mother finally gave in and Bella, the girl, runs after the family to invite them in (Terloeva 2006: chapter 17).

Bella has her own love story and Terloeva (2006: chapter 18) shares it with the reader. Bella fell in love with her brother's friend Ramzan, whom she knew had known since childhood; but, according to tradition, such love was forbidden. It could have caused Bella's bother to feel anger towards his friend, so it was wrong. Ramzan leaves for a year. When he returns, he does not treat Bella with the kindness she expects. Yet, Bella interprets Ramzan's behaviour as his internal battle between tradition and his feelings. The politics of love is manifest here in how Bella reflects on tradition which sets honour before love. She accepts that their love is forbidden. But their feelings contradict the customs,and she believes that there is a way to work this out. Bella never gets Ramzan – the war comes between them psychologically, and then physically. Ramzan could only talk about war the night he returned. When he leaves again to return to the battlefield, it is for the last time.

In Terloeva's autobiography, compassion and love intertwine. Of all the things she could have written about war, she writes entire chapters on the exper-iences of love and compassion. Milana Terloeva does not share any stories of her own romantic love life – perhaps there was nothing to share at the time – though she nonetheless concentrates on the compassion, passion and love of others. Perhaps love is her way of meeting the world, seeing the world and overcoming grief. This would be the politics of love, the generous conception of love, Hardt and Negri (2004) refer to.

Terloeva was in Moscow in 2000 and was taken to a militia station when she refused to offer bribes to an officer. While interrogating Terloeva, one militia officer, being left alone with her, suddenly starts talking about fighting in the first Chechen war. He addresses Terloeva as someone who, unlike the others, knows war. The officer explains how he went to Grozny with his cousin not knowing where they were being sent to. His cousin died there. While Terloeva remains silent, the man keeps talking about his cousin who was 20 years old, and whose only passion was football. This is a former soldier, the enemy, sharing his war experience with a Chechen woman, the victim, who is being interrogated because she refused to pay the officers.

The police officer is trying to form a connection between them by explaining that they were regular young men, not monsters. With details of his cousin's life, the officer makes known the tragic and irreplaceable loss of life. He is saying: We are human too. We suffer because of this war too. Terloeva is not willing to engage in a dialogue with the Russian officer but she writes that she feels pity for his loneliness, and utters, "I am sorry about your cousin." She is listening, carefully. When allowed to leave, Terloeva still asks, "What is your name?" "Micha," the officer answers. "And your cousin?" "Vitya." Later in the book, Terloeva tells a story about soldiers doing a cleansing operation at her university in the spring of 2001. She calls them lost soldiers who did not know what they were doing, and who were not prepared for the cruelties the Russian army practices. They were victims too.

In 2002, Terloeva started collecting testimonials from civilians with a French journalist in Grozny. One day a young man in his twenties wearing a militia uniform came in. Terloeva was surprised but then she looked at him. She writes that she had never seen such pain in a man's eyes. His entire face expressed distress. The man tells his story. He works with the Russians, but only in order to help Chechens. Because he tried to help save Chechen combatants, the Russians were headed to his home to arrest him. The man managed to escape and went to find help while his family was in the house. When he returned with ten men, his father and brother were already dead. What is so painful to the man is that he believes his father died thinking that he had abandoned them and left them to die at the hands of the Russians. He was left to take care of his brother's four children and his only wish was to get his revenge. He could not marry because his brother's children would see him love his own children more than them. He has come to tell this story because he has no one else to talk to. What he wants to say, is that not all Chechens are resistance fighters or victims. The Chechen militia can be as cruel as the Russian mercenaries. War changes people.

There are many important insights in this story. First, the pain in the eyes of the man in the militia uniform and the man's need to share his story is yet another example of a Chechen man sharing publicly his intimate feelings. Second, this story reveals the complexity of enmities: how someone will assist the enemy in order to save his own kind. Third, this story reveals much about love and loss. Terloeva says that in that 25-year-old man's body she saw the soul of a 100-year-old man. Terloeva validates the man's experiences like she validates the Russian officer's experiences. The people in Terloeva's stories escape stilling – they are not simply victims or perpetrators.

Zina and Deni Will Have Each Other

While Terloeva was studying in Paris, she met other Chechens who often talked about the war. In the autumn of 2004, she talked with a young man called Soulemaine, who proposed that, for once, they would talk about something happy. "The world can smile at us too! Even in war time!" (Terloeva 2006). Soulemaine shares a story about a divinely beautiful woman, the "heroine of the story." This story touched me so deeply it inspired several performances. Despite all the loss, love can find its way through war.

> Oh, Zina, she is beautiful. It is a day of celebration and her face is one big smile and the spring wind touches her dress. It looks like a typical wedding except ...
>
> Zina is not leaving her parent's house, but the prison gates of Rostov.
>
> But do not feel blue. For this is a story about love inside the prison walls.
> Can you imagine!
>
> While in prison the lovers don't meet, but their words meet.
> They fall in love by writing each other letters. Secretly, discretely.
>
> When Zina walks out, Deni has already been released. Waiting for her.
>
> What a happy story! It's the beginning of the second Chechen war but Zina and Deni will have each other.

In autumn 1999, an anti-terrorist operation was implemented resulting in the erroneous imprisonment of ordinary Chechens. Zina was the only Chechen woman taken to Rostov prison where Soulemaine was incarcerated. Along with two other men, Deni and Yusup, Soulemaine quickly heard the news about Zina. The men decided to contact her to protect her so that she would not feel lonely. The prisoners passed secret messages through small holes. This is how they were able to establish and keep contact with Zina without ever meeting her in person. But for Deni, Zina became someone more important, and soon all the prison knew about their romance. Deni's brother outside the prison provided him with pens and paper, and money to bribe the messengers. Deni did not reveal to his brother that he was in love, because he was already being teased by others who said, "Maybe she is ugly." But Deni would reply, "She is not ugly, and even if she was, I will still marry her."

Deni kept writing but his brother finally managed to pay for his release. He asked to be left there for another month because Zina had another 30 days left of her sentence. Deni could not go against his brother who insisted he leave the prison right away. But he wanted to stay. Returning from the visiting room, Deni finally saw Zina being escorted by the guards. She was beautiful, like Deni knew she would be. He sent her his last letter, a marriage proposal for the day she would be released from prison and Zina answered "yes." They married, and had children.

Here is a politics of love in the war context, in which love is found in an unusual place. Love gives hope, and Zina's and Deni's story is what the young need to hear when they live with the scars of war. Here is a politics of love in which gendered expectations make way for the feeling of emotions. The men in Terloeva's stories talk about heartache, and the women are not women to whom marriage happens. Even Bella's story portrays how tradition is negotiated when she reflects on how she and Ramzan should behave but how their feelings could still result in a happy end.

War transforms a person, and this transformation is fundamental in building and dismantling structures of war and peace. *Love transforms a person*, and this transformation is relevant collectively. The ways relationships are structured in societies are deeply political, and often violent. Yet it is love that is broad and open-minded about others that is transformative. It is love in multitude (Hardt and Negri 2004) and love as in-betweenness (Choi 2013). The story of Ali and Ceda does not have a happy ending, but the letter Ali writes expresses the spirituality of love. Love in his letter is not a drug, or a dependency, but a connection between individuals. Ali reveals his innermost self and expresses his debt of gratitude to Ceda, even if he is unable to change.

The aesthetics of Terloeva's narrative is what Choi (2013: 130) describes as "aesthetics that disrupts the easy alignment of bodies, objects, dreams and promises." Terloeva's book situates love in the centre of experience, even in war time. Love is not a marginal narrative. Through the complexity of love in war time, Terloeva demonstrates a queering love, to which Choi points, between embrace and standing alone. Embrace is but a fleeting moment, and by attending to the fluctuation between embrace and loneliness, Terloeva makes love central to understanding lived experiences in war. In Terloeva's stories, the loss and vulnerability of love is a constant.

Thinking of love in its multitude, there seems to be an entire national narrative of Chechen-ness built upon the loss of love, and the rebuilding of love. There is never that perfect union of the imagined community, yet love gives the necessary hope in the darkest of times. Love is always accompanied by the closeness of loss – death having her share. In her openness to otherness, Terloeva is at the intersection between love and compassion. When she is mindful of the Russian officer, listening to his stories, she needs to negotiate with her love for her people and the loss she has witnessed.

When Milana Terloeva returns to Chechnya from her studies in France, she sees fear and silence. The local militia is terrorising the population and unlike during the bombings, when the good and the bad were on different sides, the (post-)war is maybe even worse than the war. It is the *Chechenisation* of the conflict. Clean-ups continue, and it feels like the rule of Stalin to her. Corruption and the criminality of President Kadyrov are not spoken of. One wrong gesture or word, and the person disappears. Terloeva worries how the children in Chechnya will grow up, when war is all they have seen. For them, war is the normal. Will they know peace and freedom?

7

Lie

Forget-me-not objects rising from beneath,
sharing stories of lived lives of people

Handcuffed to the trees the spirits pled for mercy,
and they're numb and they regret
not rejoicing to the full
When they still had the chance
When they still had the chance

But you know they played music very loud,
and I know how they played to the night
How they played to the night

It's a lie to say I don't
It's a lie to say I won't

It's a lie to say they're dead,
when born to the painful
Cause items from beneath
are not those of the never-land

Real people held hands
They painted the walls
They cried out loud
They cried out loud

It's a lie to say I don't
It's a lie to say I won't

One last time
Floating in the air
Catch them stories

Read them aloud
And hold them dear
And hold them dear

I don't make songs about Chechnya anymore. I have not in a long time. The songs arrived in a rather compact timeframe, at a time when I realised it was one thing to study states and structures, and another to study human life. War touched, and touch could not be intellectualised or articulated with jargon.

Lie was the last one. When I took it down, sitting on my living room floor, I realised that something had changed. I no longer considered the songs separate from my own life, but began to see how I was writing from my own dark places. Lie became more personal, and once that happened, all songs became personal, and I saw them from a new perspective. That is when seeds of doubt were planted. Seeds of doubt about what I was doing in the first place. What was I singing, and why?

Returning to Ranciére (2016), art affects by defining ways of being together and being separated. The songs can be seen as defining togetherness and separateness. That is the territory where the songs move, for me. The impact of aesthetics is unpredictable – it is in the moving of bodies, the rearrangement of the sensual. The songs are a dialogue about the ethics and aesthetics of researching war. I did not only write myself in, I let the research write something on my body, and I changed.

They Painted the Walls

This book has sought aesthetic insight into lived experiences and emotions in Chechnya. The focus has been on embodiment as a research method and the body as the site of emoting. Sources included two autobiographies (Baiev et al. 2003; Terloeva 2006), three documentary films (*Barzakh*, *Children of Beslan*, *The 3 Rooms of Melancholia*), one motion picture (*12*) and interviews (with Ali and Said 2017). Film, in particular, allows a reading of the body though senses. It provides access to spaces I could not have travelled to and points of view I would not have thought of.

In the documentary film *Barzakh* (Chapter four), a woman is painting the ceiling of her house. Painting a ceiling is hard work. Arms begin to hurt after a while because you need to keep them straight up. I wonder why she is doing the painting, why not a young brisk man, for example? Are they gone, the young men who could help her? I wonder why the process of painting seems so inefficient and slow. The brush is too small for painting a ceiling, and the paint looks watery. Is she just trying to pass the time? Is she repairing something which will never be finished? Painting appears again later in the film, when men are standing in a cell where people were tortured and killed. A man tells how they had to whitewash the bloody walls and floors. Paint away with fresh white the colour of deep red blood. Paint away the proof, clean up the mess as a part of the collective punishment.

The material world is affective too, and deeply so. Remembering and forgetting are attached to places and spaces. Russian soldiers violated the homes of Chechens, looting, breaking and even defecating inside their houses or inside a mosque as Politkovskaya (2003) describes. Soldiers violated the home of Milana Terloeva (2006) too, using books as toilet paper, destroying art works and her spring dress – a violation completely unnecessary and very personal. There is nothing rational about defecating all around someone's home. Emotions are constitutive of war. The scene of the painting encapsulates the rebuilding of lives only for everything to be destroyed again. In the torture cell, the imprisoned were painting over the sins of the torturers, knowing that the walls will be covered in blood soon again. In the material realm of war, money paid for the victims in Beslan meant a calculation of how much their suffering was worth. Baiev's care for the cow Zoyka makes the reader realise that Zoyka is a dear companion to her family, a valuable life in herself, not just a provider of milk.

I began my research focussed on compassion. Compassion, which I define as embodied courage and vulnerability – a connection between individuals or groups. If we only focus on studying violence in war, we risk becoming voyeuristic and hopeless. I ended up expanding the study to include love and children's agency which I felt merited attention because the themes pushed forward from the material. Love, because it comes so close to compassion, yet has its own peculiarities through the intimacy of the relationship. Children, who are in need of protection and whose role in war can be underestimated. With this book, I have tried to emphasise how war is not something that just happens to children and to women, and suggested that we need to engage with our emotions as researchers and spectators, *with an enhanced awareness of corporeality – the kinaesthetic-emotional relationship to the other.*

In this book, I have conveyed stories of compassion as embodied. I have taken the *Bodhisattva Never Disparaging* (Chapter three) as the model of compassion which is indiscriminating and manifests corporeally. I have theorised emotion through neuroscience as emoting in the body, and through enactivism, the singularity of body and mind. This enabled me to shift attention to the far ends of the radar, to think about compassion through Khassan Baiev's hands, his miraculous rescue from the pit, and the female nurses who worked alongside him. The corporeality of compassion is exemplified in the experience of Milana Terloeva (2006) who was touched by the pain she saw in the eyes of the man who came to tell his story to the journalists. It is not just the story about the murder of his family, but his entire face which revealed suffering before the man began to talk.

In Chapter four, I took embodiment a step further by suggesting that dance can be a form and expression of compassion, as well as resistance. Bodily movement, kinaesthesia and choreography transmit emotions from the self to the other. The body is a site of powerful war experience, and the body is the site of healing. Trauma is a physical state as much as a psychological one – the entire body responds to trauma. Because the entire body needs to recover from trauma, to stop signalling danger, I propose, the dancer can tap into her own body as a site of healing, hope and also compassion. Dance and movement therapy have been developed as a means for a body-based tool for healing. In a community in which formal dance therapy is unavailable, the practice of dance can still work as a method of self-healing.

The metaphor of the eagle signifies the dancer's freedom, and freedom in general, in Chechnya. The dancer remembers and lives freedom in the moment. In the film *Barzakh*, dance brings a relief and it connects people. In the film *12*, compassion manifests through synchronous embodiment. Members of the jury remember suffering in their bodyminds while the accused young Chechen begins to embody hope through his dance. Bodies become out of joint, they change together. Emoting, rather than 'rational deliberation' causes the jury members to finally vote not guilty and abandon their prejudice. The film shows how compassion is embodied; for the jury members, compassion is not a strategy or a performance, it is lived. At the same time, *12* comments on war in Chechnya, and how war continues to be lived.

In Chapter five, the children in Beslan, Kronstedt, Grozny and Ingushetia are not reducible to representations of helpless victims. They embody agency, they form and express political opinions based on their experiences. Children, even if in need of protection, are capable individuals who affect their environments. When we categorise children through their victimhood, we can miss the important role children play in the society. If we do not listen to them or see them, we miss their insights, creativity and coping mechanisms. The scene of Hadijat taking away the children from their sick mother is an example of the difficulty that comes with judging compassion by behaviour. In war everyone is abandoned. The experience of abandonment travels from the carnal level throughout the society, all the way to the international. As Milana Terloeva (2006) writes, Chechnya was abandoned by the rest of the world. Yet, even in the most horrific conditions of war, Zina and Deni fell in love in a

Russian detention centre. In Chapter six, I discussed how relationships are broken by war, but also how love can work its way through the most challenging of circumstances. The politics of love lies in the aesthetics, arrangement and rearrangement of sensual settings. Love is a transformative power. This is why I would like to see more research on how war ruins and enables love.

Collective Emotions

Traumatic experiences weigh heavily on collective emotions. As Bleiker and Hutchison (2008a: 387) write, "We believe there is evidence to suggest that an active engagement with emotions can actually be a source of political imagination, inspiration and hope." A politics of grief then involves questioning pre-conceived ideas about how individuals and societies can best deal with past violence. Bleiker and Hutchison hope that by addressing collective emotions, it will be possible to cultivate empathy and compassion. In Chapter two, I introduced the history of war in Chechnya, and discussed how history and historical memories are part of the collective identity. As an example, Ali (2017) told me that, under Kadyrov, difficult history is being erased from the public consciousness. He tells me that in Chechnya, people are not allowed to talk about the deportations of 1944 anymore, as if they did not happen. Moreover, Kadyrov has forbidden the mourning day of February 23rd and introduced a new national holiday – a solidarity day – to be observed on May 8th, the day his father died. This is an attempt to rewrite history for the purpose of constructing a new national identity.

Overcoming collective trauma requires dealing with it openly and publicly. We have no indication that such a development is taking place in Russia. The Russian government has denied atrocities such as abductions and torture, and families affected have had very little possibility to seek redress through the domestic judicial system (Van der Vet 2013). They have had to file applications to the European Court of Human Rights with the help of NGOs. Amnesty International (2009) stated with regards to the decision by Russia to end the counter-terrorism operation in Chechnya, that, "normalization is not possible without full accountability for the gross human rights violations of the last 10 years." Acknowledging, commemorating and remembering are important. There is no such climate or political space in Russia or Chechnya in which emotions and trauma could be collectively engaged with. There is no space in which collective fear could give way to healing.

Hutchison (2016) writes about collective trauma as a social phenomenon beyond individual PTSD. Collective trauma affects how people and governments perceive security issues and identities. Trauma isolates individuals but it also shapes political communities. Hutchison (2016: 4) refers to *affective community*, a community welded together by shared emotional understanding of a tragedy. In the case of Chechnya, collective trauma has a long history. Resistance, endless hope and tradition have been seen as the only means to survive as a people. Shaming is part of that heritage although shame is not something that helps people survive, but the contrary. Shame isolates and traumatises, in Chechnya and elsewhere. Shame is the dark side of vulnerability and a hindrance to healing and compassion.

Compassion is a central social emotion, and thus important for understanding war experience. I regard compassion, kindness and love in war as forms of resistance because they provide hope as opposed to fear, anger and resentment – emotions typically associated with war (see Petersen 2011). Baiev helping the Russian doctor Sasha escape is an example of grassroots resistance to war and its affective economy (Baiev et al. 2003). Chechen wedding dance is an example of how people do not let war defeat them or let resentment and fear define them. Despite the stillness of the scenes in *Barzakh*, Chechens dance at a wedding.

One can dismiss examples presented in this study as anomalies which require no paradigm change. We can keep to disembodied readings of politics, see the private experience as irrelevant to the larger structures of war and politics, and narrow the study of war as lived experience to pain and suffering. But neuroscientist V. S. Ramachandran writes about how he typically studied only a few patients but ended up discovering more than just the particularities of individual cases; he learned things that helped him formulate general theories about perception, memory and consciousness (Ramachandran and Blakeslee 1998). One person who manifests compassion in war is not an anomaly – she is proof of the capacity of the human being. Perhaps by looking into compassion, love and vulnerability, we can learn also about collective emotions related to experiences of war. Through this we can develop more practices which promote peaceful co-existence.

Collective emotions are, in my view, wonderfully visible in the choreography of Chechen dance. The dancer and the spectator both participate in the production of knowledge and insight. Dancing raises the possibility of remembering the forgotten self, and the synchronised tapping of hands at a wedding produces muscular bonding and potentially, well-being. Rhythm is collective, it means attuning the inside with the outside. Synchronous movement between bodies has been shown in clinical trials to induce compassion, yet we need to investigate muscular bonding specifically in the context of war and conflict – a challenge I am embarking on next. Involuntary, or non-conscious, bonding can be excited through collective movement – I call it the boundless body not because bodies become one, but because people are touched by each other throughout the body whether they like it or not.

During this research, I have come to see compassion as something ordinary, subtle and discreet. One does not have to be a heroic individual in order to be compassionate, although some individuals seem to be extraordinarily brave. It is easy to look at the lives and stories of people who have become famous for their activism. Yet, compassion is not a state of exception or the quality of some supreme individuals, but part of daily life and even mundane encounters – the ability to meet other bodies in dance, to discuss with other bodies in the war context, to show vulnerability, to see another person, to enjoy what there is to enjoy, to laugh, to clap hands and tap feet, to submerge in the dance – resists conflictual and violent meetings between bodies.

Bleiker and Hutchison (2008a) write that dealing with the trauma of war is a major political challenge. Reconciliation requires conscious political engagement with complicated collective emotions. What I suggest here is that we need to know what to look for when we want to engage with compassion. How we excite compassion and alleviate suffering depends on our understanding of what compassion is and how it is embodied. The question is not only about how political elites can advocate for compassion, or how they can make compassionate policies, but how compassion can take root in people amidst war. Traumatic events can, in fact, pull people together, as Bleiker and Hutchison write. In order to stop the spiralling cycles of violence, collective emotions need to be addressed. Traumatic memories are passed down from one generation to the next, not only socially-politically but even genetically. For example, during and after war, children are born with disabilities caused by pollution from the war but also the stress and PTSD symptoms experienced by pregnant mothers. Emotions are not just personal, but we begin to comprehend collective emotions when we analyse at the micro-level.

Milana Terloeva's grandmother, who lived through Stalin's deportations, said to her granddaughter, "We will rebuild, like we always do. We have no right to despair. We are condemned to hope" (Terloeva 2006). How did Terloeva maintain hope in the aftermath of the second war? By going to the destroyed, but still standing, Grozny University, like so many other youth. They tried to create an illusion of normality. The children and youth affected by war craved everything ordinary. Education was an ordinary privilege even though it posed serious risks. Despite the ruins and sadness all around, Terloeva looks back on her student years in Grozny as happy times.

Wanting normalcy after a traumatic event is not about denying trauma or the need to mourn. In Beslan, the families could not continue their lives because life was stolen from them. The families in *Barzakh* could not continue living either because they hoped that the stolen lives would be returned one day. They kept searching, filing papers and waiting. So the woman keeps painting the ceiling with the small brush and watery paint. The fact that Milana Terloeva went to her beloved university is an embodiment of hope. Keeping to the illusion of normalcy was to have hope. There would be a future.

Their War, Our Music

> [...] love and hate and anguish, the qualities of kindness and cruelty, the planned solution of a scientific problem or the creation of a new artefact are all based on neural events within a brain, provided that brain has been and now is interacting with its body. The soul breathes through the body, and suffering, whether it starts in the skin or in a mental image, happens in the flesh (Damasio 1995: xvii).

I believe it is of the utmost importance to value corporeal knowledge in science and in daily life. It is not even radical to be curious about the way the body moves, breathes and is. The body dances and it kills, and immersing oneself in the aesthetics of the body can lead to hidden insights. Bodily awareness is ordinary in many disciplines and practices. For some reason, the real living tissue seems to be off-limits for International Relations, unless it is studied as an object of politics – an *object body* – controlled, influenced, hurt, and acted upon. Yet, as an observer of aesthetics, there is no path to a discovery of the authentic lived body. To get to know the subject body, it would be necessary to interview people about their felt states. Such interviews were not possible in this study.

We act through the body. We act through the body as researchers too. As we act, we feel. As we feel, we act. As we perceive, we remember. As we remember, we perceive. We emote all the time. When I take my own body on stage, I take a risk. Every single time I perform, I come back to the questions: What are these songs supposed to mean? What are they supposed to do? Then I ask myself, *how* can I sing about war? Should I convey melancholy and sadness? War is about suffering after all. But my study is not, and people can dance to this music. So I never really wanted the listener to feel sadness, sorrow, guilt, or pity. To feel compassion, yes, and to begin to think anew.

We experience through an interaction of bodies, our lives are not separate and wholly private. We can never see what the other person is seeing, or feel what she is feeling – that is the private experience – but we never experience anything fully alone. Our experiences are interactions with the environment which includes all living beings we encounter. It is not only the mind-body separation that is problematic, but the separation of self from the environment is yet another illusion. When this illusion is shattered, we can see how war affects everyone – war travels within experiences and narratives through space and time.

I have taken this research through art outside the academic context. I have taken the songs to peace and discussion events, to bars and concert stages. These moments themselves have become pieces of art. These practices have also enabled randomness and the spontaneous participation of people from different walks of life. As an example, I gave my mobile phone to a spectator to film my performance which makes that person part of the artistic work (see: https://www.susannahast.com/sounds-of-war). This particular video is for a piece I made called *Dark place / Bright place* from a Valentine's Day peace walk event in Helsinki in February 2016. The idea was to narrate war but without offering an auditory representation of suffering. I used more cheerful music with the narration on violence (the dark place), and darker sounds for the part that takes the listener to a bright place. I wanted to suggest a different affective state with the text and the melody because, as Rancière (2008) suggests, aesthetic influence is a conflict between different orders of sensing. I wanted to prove that the body and the melody are involved in the emotional meaning-making then and there. I wondered if the listener would be disturbed by the conflict between narration and melody. But to my surprise, someone in the audience told me afterwards that it was easier to listen to the violent stories because of the funky melody. The melody made listening to the lyrics tolerable. That is, the melody and text together created a learning experience.

The point of researching war is not voyeurism, and research does not need to focus on violent images and stories. Research should provoke thought, sensibility and kindness. Then the performance becomes a dialogue in which the performer is willing to be seen, and the audience has the patience to participate. As I stated in the first chapter, research methods, theories and even scientific communication intertwine. I try to practise what I preach: connection. Later I received similar feedback – that the songs have an impact because they might not be easy or comfortable to listen to when you know the background. If successful, performance becomes an exercise in vulnerability and an analysis of power structures. When I perform, I am no longer arguing or educating, but I am still producing embodied insights. Doing art, I notice, I am doing research. I am making research and artistic practice ontologically one. This practice is not about self-indulgence, it is about making myself a political subject. Moreover, I could not do this alone.

Our music is like an unnatural soundtrack to a war experience which is not mine. The music in this book is not about the authentic voices of war; it is an aesthetic addition to a soundscape of war. Songwriting and performance are acts negotiating difference. It is not my war, but my body singing. The songs exist as if in-between bodies. As I perform, my body becomes so political it hurts. I keep thinking, what have I got the musicians playing with me into. They did not do the research with me, but on stage, they are doing the research with me. I want to smile, but I stop myself because it feels wrong. I want to dance, but that also feels weird. For a moment, I lose myself in the music, but then return to an uncomfortable state. I think of Baiev and how it felt wrong for him to listen to music in the hospital because it would seem like they were having fun. The body follows the beat, and there is nothing wrong with that. I wanted to make songs that inspire the body to move.

In the course of this research I have come to understand that in music, science and art meet spirituality. I believe spirituality helps to overcome the shame that can come from making oneself vulnerable. Throughout this project of understanding compassion, shame has been my loyal friend and dear companion. There are many practical implications for shame, but what they have in common is hiding. Shame is an ethos of our time, and yet it is invisible. Shame silences, prevents dancing and turns some people into killers. Shame is fundamentally political and in many ways gendered. Shame gives structure to power relations and defines good scholarship. When I wrote *Pit* I was not thinking about ever performing it. There was nothing perform-ative about the song and so there was no shame. I simply felt joy from the creative process. The people who shared their stories overcame the shame they might have felt from being seen and known. This is a politics of com-passion. These stories are vulnerability's good side. I have merely tried to collect and tie the stories together. We need to make these stories visible because we need to understand different points of view if we are to imagine alternatives to violence. Those in power must not be the only ones allowed to create knowledge. I am concerned over my own use of power in the position of the specialist. I began songwriting because when I present myself as a singer, I give up the authority of the academic. This manifests concretely when my performance is not taken as scholarship, and when I am not referred to as a researcher while performing.

Sounds of Compassion

We are musical beings. The art of storytelling is common to music and science. In order to speak about music-making as a research practice together with the political, a new word was needed and it is *musistance*, or musical resistance. Musistance challenges sterile and disembodied academic ideals. Musistance makes passion central to the production of embodied insights. It challenges the binaries of body/mind and thinking/feeling. Musistance breaks the boundaries of theory, methodology and analysis.

I now realise that art is not just a methodology or the object of study, but the heart beating, the essence and the edge of things. It is not just that art talks to reality, constructs it or interprets it, but that reality itself is artistic. Reality itself is poetic, musical, rhythmical and pictorial. Dissolving the boundaries and borders of art, science and reality are practices. I cannot work my way through it in language alone. I have tried to be as direct and honest as possible in my writing because music creates connections, and vulnerability is the space in which I need to move as a researcher. The songs are the heart beating in this research, and nothing I say or write expresses the heart, the essence, the edge quite like the songs.

I cannot claim to have an ethical relationship to my object of study because I do not know how to eliminate power, or what a truly equal collaboration or consideration for the other looks like. Something which started from intuition has had to be reasoned later, and that reasoning has limitations. I have had to invent explanations of songwriting, which were not there when I wrote the songs. The songs haunt me, because I am haunted by the stories and images of people's experiences in war. Singing is my attempt to underline a spiritual, uncanny, 'not knowing' part of research to treasure, not hide or deny. I hope one day I can transmit my own experience of songwriting as a practice to someone who needs it.

The songs are a witness of war, a witness of conviction, a hopeful witness. Musistance is political and it relies on the affective power music. This affective power is why music has been a tool of propaganda and resistance alike – music moves and motivates people. Music speaks and communicates directly with the body – it is carnal knowledge that expresses the unsaid. Music creates connections and is an exercise in vulnerability. Vulnerability is a space of resistance and compassion. Music underlines how deeply human we are.

Musistance is having the imagination to shift the focus from the study of illness to the good which is already there. Musistance is a human revolution, subverting hegemonic and violent practices in IR in favour of a view of the body situated as part of the world. Musistance is a politics of love and compassion which emerged from encounters with the heaven of life amidst the hell of war in Chechnya. We need this human revolution of love and compassion because structural changes are never enough if the human heart remains corrupt. I call this book *Sounds of War*, but it is even more so a book about the sounds of compassion. Because, *we are all condemned to hope*.

References

Akhmadov, Ilyas and Miriam Lanskoy. 2010. *The Chechen Struggle: Independence Won and Lost*. New York: Palgrave Macmillan.

Amnesty International. 2009. "No progress in Chechnya without accountability." *Amnesty International*, 17 April. Accessed 1 May 2017. https://www.amnesty.org/en/latest/news/2009/04/no-avances-chechenia-sin-rendicion-cuentas-20090417/

Ankersmit, Frank. 1997. *Aesthetic Politics: Political Philosophy Beyond Fact and Value*. Stanford: Stanford University Press.

Anttila, Eeva. 2007. "Mind the Body: Unearthing the Affiliation between the Conscious Body and the Reflective Mind." In *Ways of Knowing in Dance and Art*, edited by Leena Rouhiainen, 77–99. Helsinki: Theatre Academy.

Anttila, Eeva. 2013. *Koko koulu tanssii! Kehollisen oppimisen mahdollisuuksia kouluyhteisössä*. (in Finnish) Helsinki: Esittävien taiteiden tutkimuskeskus (Tutke) / Forskningscentrum för teater, dans och performance / Performing Arts Research Centre.

Ahmed, Sara. 2004a. "Affective Economies." *Social Text* 22(2): 117–139.

Ahmed, Sara. 2004b. *Cultural Politics of Emotion*. Edinburg: Edinburg University Press.

Ahmed, Sara. 2004c. "Declarations of Whiteness: The Non-Performativity of Anti-Racism." *Borderlands* 3(2). Accessed 1 May 2017. http://www.borderlands.net.au/vol3no2_2004/ahmed_declarations.htm

Ahmed, Sara. 2017. *Living a Feminist Life*. Durham: Duke University Press.

Arendt, Hannah. 1958. *The Human Condition*. Chicago: The University of Chicago Press, 1998.

Åhäll, Linda. 2016. "The Dance of Militarisation: a Feminist Security Studies Take on the Political." *Critical Studies on Security* 4(2): 154-168.

Åhäll, Linda and Thomas Gregory. 2015. "Introduction: Mapping Emotions, Politics and War." In *Emotions, Politics and War*, edited by Linda Åhäll and Thomas Gregory, 1–14. New York: Routledge.

Baiev, Khassan, Ruth Daniloff and Nicholas Daniloff. 2003. *The Oath: A Surgeon under Fire.* Walker & Company: New York.

Banes, Erin K. 2015. "Today, I Want to Speak Out the Truth: Victim Agency, Responsibility, and Transitional Justice." *International Political Sociology* 9(4): 316–32.

Basham, Victoria. 2011. "Kids with Guns: Militarization, Masculinities, Moral Panic and (Dis)Organised Violence." In *The Militarization of Childhood: Thinking beyond the Global South* edited by Beier J. Marshall, 175–194. New York: Palgrave MacMillan.

Berlant, Lauren. 2004. "Introduction: Compassion (and Withholding)." In *Compassion: the Culture and Politics of an Emotion,* edited by Lauren Berlant. New York and London: Routledge, 1–13.

Berlant, Lauren. 2011. "A Properly Political Concept of Love: Three Approaches in Ten Pages." Cultural Anthropology 26(4): 683–691.

Berger, Kathleen Strassen. 2008. *The Developing Person through Childhood and Adolescence*. New York: Worth Publishers.

Bleiker, Roland. 2001. "The Aesthetic Turn in International Political Theory." *Millennium* 30(3): 509–33.

Bleiker, Roland. 2003. "Learning from Art: A Reply to Holden's World Literature and World Politics." *Global Society* 17(4): 415–28.

Bleiker, Roland. 2009. *Aesthetics and World Politics*. Basingstoke: Palgrave Macmillan.

Bleiker, Roland. 2017. "In Search of Thinking Space: Reflections on the Aesthetic Turn in International Political Theory." *Millenium* 45(2): 258–264.

Bleiker, Roland and Morgan Brigg. 2010. "Autoethonographic International Relations: Exploring the Self as a Source of Knowledge." *Review of International Studies* 36(3): 779–98.

Bleiker, Roland and Emma Hutchison. 2015. "Grief and the Transformation of Emotions after War." In *Emotions, Politics and War*, edited by Linda Åhäll and Thomas Gregory, 210–221. New York: Routledge.

Bleiker, Roland and Emma Hutchison. 2008a. "Emotional Reconciliation: Reconstructing Identity and Community after Trauma." *European Journal of Social Theory* 11(3): 385–403.

Bleiker, Roland and Emma Hutchison. 2008b. "Fear No More: Emotions and World Politics." *Review of International Studies* 34: 115–135.

Borgdorff, Henk. 2011. "The Production of Knowledge in Artistic Research." In *The Routledge Companion to Research in the Arts,* edited by Michael Biggs and Henrik Karlsson, 44–63. London: Routledge.

Brennan, Teresa. 2004. *The Transmission of Affect.* Ithaca and London: Cornell University Press.

Brown, Brené. 2010. *The Gifts of Imperfection: Let Go of Who You Think You're Supposed to Be and Embrace Who You Are.* Minnesota: Hazelden.

Brown, Brené. 2012. *The Power of Vulnerability: Teachings of Authenticity, Connection, and Courage.* Audible. Audiobook.

Burleigh, Michael. 2008. *Blood and Rage: A Cultural History of Terrorism.* London: Harper.

Butler, Judith. 2004. *Undoing Gender.* New York and London: Routledge.

Butler, Judith. 2009. *Frames of War: When is Life Grievable?.* London and New York: Verso.

Butler, Sally and Roland Bleiker. 2017. "Embodied Witnessing: Indigenous Performance Art as Political Dissent." In *Art as a Political Witness*, edited by Kia Lindroos and Frank Möller, 99–118. Opladen: Barbara Budrich Publishers.

Cacioppo, Stephanie, Haotian Zhou, George Monteleone, Elizabeth Majka, Kimberly A. Quinn, Aaron B. Ball, Greg Norman, Gün R. Semin and John T. Cacioppo. 2014. "You are in sync with me: neural correlates of interpersonal synchrony with a partner." *Neuroscience* 277: 842–58.

Chiba, Shin. 1995. "Hannah Arendt on Love and the Political: Love, Friendship, and Citizenship." *The Review of Politics* 57(3): 505–535.

Choi, Shine. 2013. "Love's Cruel Promises: Love, Unity and North Korea." *International Feminist Journal of Politics* (ahead of print): 1–18.

Chowdhury, Elora Halim. 2016. "War, Healing, and Trauma: Reading the Feminine Aesthetics and Politics in Rubaiyat Hossain's Meherjaan." *Feminist Formations* 28(3): 27–45.

Coch, Donna, Geraldine Dawson and Kurt W. Fischer. 2007. *Human Behavior, Learning, and the Developing Brain: Atypical Development.* New York and London: The Gulford Press.

Colombetti, Giovanna. 2014. *The Feeling Body: Affective Science Meets the Enactive Mind.* Cambridge, Massachusetts: The MIT Press.

Connolly, William E. 2002. *Neuropolitics: Thinking, Culture, Speed.* Minneapolis: University of Minnesota Press.

Coole, Diana and Samantha Frost. 2010. "Introducing the New Materialisms." In *New Materialism: Ontology, Agency, and Politics,* edited by Diana Coole and Samantha Frost, 1–43. Durham: Duke University Press.

Crawford, Neta C. 2014. "Institutionalizing Passion in World Politics: Fear and Empathy." *International Theory* 6(3): 535–57.

Crawford, Neta C. 2015. "Preface." In *Emotions, Politics and War*, edited by Linda Åhäll and Thomas Gregory, xvi–xxi. New York: Routledge.

D'Aloia, Anthony. 2012. "Cinematic Empathy: Spectator Involvement in the Film Experience." In *Kinesthetic Empathy in Creative and Cultural Practices,* edited by Dee Reynolds and Matthew Reason, 91–108. Bristol and Chicago: Intellect.

Daigle, Megan. 2016. "Writing the Lives of Others: Storytelling and International Politics." *Millenium* 45(1): 25–42.

Damasio, Antonio. 1995. *Descartes' Error: Emotion, Reason and the Human Brain*. New York: Avon Books.

Damasio, Antonio. 2009. "When Emotions Make Better Decisions." *Fora.tv*. YouTube. Accessed 15 January 2017. https://www.youtube.com/watch?v=1wup_K2WN0I

Damasio, Antonio. 2010. *Self Comes to Mind: Constructing the Conscious Brain*. London: William Heinemann. Kindle ed.

Daughtry, Martin J. 2015. *Listening to War: Sound, Music, Trauma, and Survival in Wartime Iraq*. Oxford: Oxford University Press.

Davies, James and Dimitrina Spencer. 2010. *Emotions in the Field: The Psychology and Anthropology of Fieldwork Experience*. Stanford: Stanford University Press.

Dauphinée, Elizabeth. 2007. *The Ethics of Researching War: Looking for Bosnia*. Manchester: Manchester University Press.

Dauphinée, Elizabeth. 2013. "Writing As Hope." *Security Dialogue* 44(3): 347–361.

De Botton, Alain. 2016. *The Course of Love: A Novel*. New York: Simon & Schuster.

Derluguian, Georgi. 2003. "Introduction: Whose Truth?" In *A Small Corner of Hell: Dispatches from Chechnya*, by Anna Politkovskaya, 1–25. Chicago and London: The University of Chicago Press.

Dodds, Klaus. 2015. "Popular Geopolitics and War on Terror." In *Popular Culture and World Politics: Theories, Methods, Pedagogies*, edited by Federica Caso and Caitlin Hamilton, 51–62. Bristol: E-International Relations.

Dyvik, Synne L. 2016. "'Valhalla rising': Gender, Embodiment and Experience in Military Memoirs." *Security Dialogue* 47(2): 133–150.

European Asylum Support Office. 2014. "Country of Origin Information Report: Chechnya. Women, Marriage, Divorce and Child Custody." *European Asylum Support Office*. Accessed 16 January 2017. https://www.easo.europa.eu/news-events/chechnya-focus-easo-published-country-origin-information-coi-report-chechnya

Eichler, Maya. 2011. "Russian Veterans of the Chechen Wars: A Feminist Analysis of Militarized Masculinities." In *Feminist International Relations: Conversations about the Past, Present and Future*, edited by J. Ann Tickner and Laura Sjoberg, 123–40. Oxon, New York: Routledge.

Enloe, Cynthia. 2000. *Maneuvers: The International Politics of Militarizing Women's Lives*. Berkeley: University of California Press.

Enloe, Cynthia. 2004. *The Curious Feminist: Searching for Women in a New Age of Empire*. Berkeley: University of California Press.

Enloe, Cynthia. 2014a. *Bananas, Beaches and Bases: Making Feminist Sense of International Politics*. 2nd ed. Berkeley: University of California Press.

Enloe, Cynthia. 2014b. "Disposable Life." *Histories of Violence*. Vimeo. Accessed 15 January 2017. https://vimeo.com/85726222

Ensler, Eve. 2013. *In the Body of the World.* New York: Metropolitan Books.

Ewart, Ewa. 2009. "The Children of Beslan Five Years On." *BBC*, 29 August. Accessed 16 January 2017. http://news.bbc.co.uk/2/hi/programmes/newsnight/8227119.stm

Eysenck, Michael W. 2012. *Fundamentals of Cognition*. Hove and New York: Psychology Press.

Fisher, Helen. 2008. "The Brain in Love." *TED*. Accessed 11 April 2017. https://www.ted.com/talks/helen_fisher_studies_the_brain_in_love/transcript

Fitzgerald, Des. 2013. "The Affective Labour of Autism Neuroscience: Entangling Emotions, Thoughts and Feelings in a Scientific Research Practice." *Subjectivity* 6(2): 131–52.

Foster, Susan 2010. *Choreographing Empathy: Kinesthesia in Performance*. New York: Routledge.

Gaensbauer, Theodore J. 2011. "Embodied Simulation, Mirror Neurons and the Reenactment of Trauma in Early Childhood." *Neuropsychoanalysis* 13(1): 91–107.

Gibbon, Jill. 2010. "Dilemmas of Drawing War." In *Experiencing War,* edited by Christine Sylvester, 103–17. New York and Oxon: Routledge.

Gilligan, Emma. 2010. *Terror in Chechnya: Russia and the Tragedy of Civilians in War.* Princeton: Princeton University Press.

Green, Jill. 2002. "Somatic knowledge: The body as content and methodology in dance education." *Journal of Dance Education* 2(4), 114–118.

Goetz, Jennifer, Dacher Keltner, Emiliana Simon-Thomas. 2010. "Compassion: An Evolutionary Analysis and Empirical Review." *Psychological Bulletin* 136 (3): 351–374.

Goodall, Jane and Phillip Berman. 2000. *Reasons for Hope: A Spiritual Journey.* New York: Warner Books.

Gorbunova, Yulia. 2017. "We Have Nothing Else to Sell but Our Teeth:

Chechens Seeking Asylum in Poland." *Human Rights Watch*, March 7. Accessed 17 July 2017. https://www.hrw.org/news/2017/03/07/we-have-nothing-else-sell-our-teeth

Habibi, Assal and Antonio Damasio. 2014. "Music, Feelings, and the Human Brain." *Psychomusicology: Music, Mind and Brain* 24(1): 92–102.

Haidt, Jonathan. 2000. "The Emotional Dog and Its Rational Tail: A Social Intuitionist Approach to Moral Judgement." *Psychological Review*, 108(4): 814–34.

Hamington, Maurice. 2004. *Embodied Care: Jane Addams, Maurice Merleau-Ponty, and Feminist Ethics*. Urbana and Chicago: University of Illinois Press.

Hanna, Judith Lynne. 2015. *Dancing to Learn: The Brain's Cognition, Emotion and Movement*. Lanham: Rowman & Littlefield.

Hardt, Michael and Antonio Negri. 2004. *Multitude: War and Democracy in the Age of Empire*. New York: The Penguin Press.

Hast, Susanna. 2014. "Creativity and the Study of Emotions: Perspective of an International Relations Scholar." *Academic Quarter: Journal of Research from the Humanities* 9: 139–50.

Hast, Susanna. 2016. "Sounds of Silence: Reflections on Songwriting and International Relations." *Critical Military Studies* 2(1-2): 133–136.

Hast, Susanna. 2017. Children Witnessing War: Emotions in the Theatre Play Wij/Zij." In *Art as a Political Witness*, edited by Kia Lindroos and Frank Möller, 199–218. Opladen: Barbara Budrich Publishers.

Hayes, Amy and Steven Tipper. 2012. "Affective Responses to Everyday Actions." In *Kinesthetic Emapthy in Creative and Cultural Practices,* edited by Dee Reynolds and Matthew Reason, 69–84. Bristol and Chicago: Intellect.

Hesford, Wendy S. 2011. *Spectacular Rhetorics: Human Rights Visions, Recognitions, Feminisms*. Durham: Duke University Press.

Hietanen, Jari K., Enrico Glerean, Riitta Hari and Lauri Nummenmaa. 2016. "Bodily Maps of Emotions across Child Development." *Developmental Science* 19(6): 1111–1118.

Hille, Kathrin. 2015. "Ramzan Kadyrov: Chechen warlord accused of brutal rule." *Financial Times,* 3 May. Accessed 1 May 2017. https://www.ft.com/content/a9db4746-ef08-11e4-87dc-00144feab7de?segmentid=acee4131-99c2-09d3-a635-873e61754ec6

Hoggett, Paul and Thompson, Simon. 2012. *"Introduction."* In *Politics and the Emotions: The Affective Turn in Contemporary Political Studies*, edited by Simon Thompson and Paul Hoggett, 1–20. New York & London: Continuum.

Hongisto, Ilona. 2015. *Soul of the Documentary: Framing, Expression, Ethics*. Amsterdam: Amsterdam University Press.

hooks, bell. 2001. *All About Love: New Visions*. New York: Perennial.

Human Rights Watch. 2006. "Widespread torture in the Chechen Republic: Human Rights Watch briefing paper for the 37th session UN Committee against Torture." *Human Rights Watch*. Accessed 16 January 2017. http://reliefweb.int/report/russian-federation/widespread-torture-chechen-republic-human-rights-watch-briefing-paper-37th

Human Rights Watch. 2005. "Worse Than a War: 'Disappearances' in Chechnya—a Crime Against Humanity." *Human Rights Watch*. Briefing Paper. Accessed 22 March 2017.https://www.hrw.org/legacy/backgrounder/eca/chechnya0305/chechnya0305.pdf

Human Rights Watch. 2000. "War Crimes in Chechnya and the Response of the West."

Human Rights Watch. Testimony before the Senate Committee on Foreign Relations. Accessed 1 May 2017. https://www.hrw.org/news/2000/02/29/war-crimes-chechnya-and-response-west

Hutchison, Emma. 2014. "A Global Politics of Pity? Disaster Imagery and the Emotional Construction of Solidarity after the 2004 Asian Tsunami." *International Political Sociology* 8(1), 1–19.

Hutchison, Emma. 2016. *Affective Communities in World Politics: Collective Emotions after Trauma*. Cambridge University Press.

Iacoboni, Marco. 2013. "The Potential of Mirror Neurons in the Contagion of Violence." In *Contagion of Violence: Workshop Summary*, Institute of Medicine and National Research Council. Washington, DC: The National Academies Press. Accessed August 10, 2017. https://www.ncbi.nlm.nih.gov/books/NBK207238/

Ilyasov, Lecha. 2009. *The Diversity of the Chechen Culture: From Historical Roots to the Present*. Ziya Bazhayev Charity Foundation.

Inayatullah, Naeem, ed. 2011. *Autobiographical International Relations*. Oxon: Routledge.

Inayatullah, Naeem and Elizabeth Dauphinée, eds. 2016. *Narrative Global Politics: Theory, History and the Personal in International Relations*. Oxon: Routledge.

Jaimoukha, Amjad. 2005. *The Chechens: A Handbook*. London and New York: Routledge.

Jeffery, Renée. 2014. "The Promise and Problems of the Neuroscientific Approach to Emotions." *International Theory* 6(3): 584–589.

Johnson, Mark. 2007. *Meaning of the Body: Aesthetics of Human Understanding*. Chicago and London: The University of Chicago Press.

Johnston, Hank. 2008. "Ritual, Strategy, and Deep Culture in the Chechen National Movement." *Critical Studies on Terrorism* 1(3): 321–342.

Kalat, James W. 2008. *Biological Psychology.* Wadsworth: Cengage Learning.

Klien, Michael, Steve Valk and Jeffrey Gormly. 2008. *Book of Recommendations: Choreography as an Aesthetics of Change*. Limerick: Daghda Dance Company.

Knowles, J. Gary and Ardra L.Cole. 2008. *Handbook of the Arts in Qualitative Research: Perspectives, Methodologies, Examples, and Issues*. Los Angeles: Sage.

Kotilainen, Noora. 2016. *Visual Theatres of Suffering: Constituting the Western Spectator in the Age of the Humanitarian World Politics.* Helsinki: University of Helsinki. Doctoral dissertation.

Kvedaravicius, Mantas. 2012. *Knots of absence: death, dreams, and disappearances at the limits of law in the Counter-Terrorism Zone of Chechnya*. Doctoral dissertation. University of Cambridge.

Lamott, Anne. 1995. *Bird by Bird: Instructions on Writing and Life*. Audible. Audiobook.

Lasarati, Rachmi Diyah. 2013. *The Dance That Makes You Vanish: Cultural Reconstruction in Post-Genocide Indonesia*. Minnesota: University of Minnesota Press.

Launay, Jaques, Roger T. Dean and Freya Bailes. 2014. "Synchronising Movements with the Sounds of a Virtual Partner Enhances Partner Likeability." *Cognitive Processing* 15(4): 491–501.

Laurén, Anna-Lena. 2009. *Vuorilla ei ole herroja: Kaukasiasta ja sen kansoista*. Helsinki: Teos & Söderström.

Leavy, Patricia. 2015. *Method Meets Art: Art-Based Research Practice*. The Guilford Press. Kindle ed.

Levine, Peter A. and Ann Frederick. 1997. *Walking the Tiger: Healing Trauma*. Berkley: North Atlantic Books.

Lewis Herman, Judith. 2011. *Trauma and Recovery: The Aftermath of Violence from Domestic Abuse to Political Terror*. Audible. Audiobook.

Lindroos, Kia and Frank Möller. 2017. *Art as a Political Witness*. Opladen: Barbara Budrich Publishers.

Lumsden, Joanne, Lynden K. Miles and C. Neil Macrae. 2014. "Sync or Sink? Interpersonal Synchrony Impacts Self-Esteem." *Frontiers in Psychology* 5.

MacKenzie, Sarah K. 2008. "Aesthetically Pleasing, but it's (not) Research: Responding Poetically to a Question of Methodology." *Forum: Qualitative Social Research Sozialforschung* 9(2). Accessed 1 May 2017. http://www. qualitative-research.net/index.php/fqs/article/view/401

Macmillan, Lorraine. 2011. "Militarized Children and Sovereign Power." In *The Militarization of Childhood: Thinking beyond the Global South*, edited by Beier J.Marshall, 61-76. New York: Palgrave MacMillan.

McNeill, W.H. 1995. *Keeping Together in Time: Dance and Drill in Human History*. Cambridge and Massachusetts: Harvard University Press.

Manning, Erin. 2007. *Politics of Touch: Sense, Movement, Sovereignty*. Minneapolis: University of Minnesota Press.

Manovski, Miroslav Pavle. 2014. *Arts-Based Research, Autoethnography and Music Education: Singing Through a Culture of Marginalization*. Rotterdam: Sense Publishers.

Marcotte, Amanda. 2016. "Overcompensation Nation: It's time to admit that toxic masculinity drives gun violence." *Salon*, 13 June. Accessed 16 2017. http://www.salon.com/2016/06/13/overcompensation_nation_its_time_to_ admit_that_toxic_masculinity_drives_gun_violence/

Martin, Rosemary. 2016. "Dancing in the Spring: Dance, Hegemony, and Change." In *Choreographies of the 21st Century Wars*, edited by Gay Morris and Jens Richard Giersdorf, 207–222. New York: Oxford University Press.

McNiff, Shaun. 2008. "Art-Based Research." In *Handbook of the Arts in Qualitative Research: Perspectives, Methodologies, Examples, and Issues*, edited by J. Gary Knowles and Ardra L.Cole, 29–41. Los Angeles: Sage.

Médecins Sans Frontières. 1999. "Chechnya: The Tracking of Civilians: Interviews with Chechen Refugees in Georgia." *Médecins Sans Frontières*. Accessed 30 December 2016. http://speakingout.msf.org/ru/node/2655

Médecins Sans Frontières. 2014. "War crimes and politics of terror in Chechnya 1994-2004." Médecins Sans Frontières. Accessed 30 December 2016. http://speakingout.msf.org/en/war-crimes-and-politics-of-terror-in-chechnya

Merleau-Ponty, Maurice. 1964. *The Primacy of Perception*. Northwestern University Press.

Merrell, Floyd. 2003. *Sensing Corporeally: Toward a Posthumanist Understanding*. Toronto, Buffalo, London: University of Toronto Press.

Mills, Dana. 2017. "The Body Remembers: Dance, Discourse of Citizenship, Phenomenology and Memory." In *Art as a Political Witness*, edited by Kia Lindroos and Frank Möller, 65–78. Opladen: Barbara Budrich Publishers.

Milton, Cynthia E. 2017. "Art as Remembrance and Trance in Post-Conflict Latin America." In *Art as a Political Witness*, edited by Kia Lindroos and Frank Möller, 117–138. Opladen: Barbara Budrich Publishers.

Mirovalev, Mansur. 2015. "Chechnya's hard-line protector of Muslim rights." *Aljazeera,* 1 October. Accessed 1 May 2017. http://www.aljazeera.com/indepth/features/2015/10/chechnya-hard-line-protector-muslim-rights-151001085135746.html

Mollica, Richard F. 2009. *Healing Invisible Wounds: Paths to Hope and Recovery in a Violent World*. Nashville: Vanderbilt University Press.

Monni, Kirsi. 1995. "Avoimet mahdollisuudet. Kehon henkisyys, hengen kehollisuus." In *Esiintyjä: Taiteen tulkki ja tekijä* edited by Raija Ojala (in Finnish), 63–74. Porvoo: WSOY.

Morris, Gay and Jens Richard Giersdorf. 2016. "Introduction." In *Choreographies of the 21st Century Wars*, edited by Gay Morris and Jens Richard Giersdorf, 1–24. New York: Oxford University Press.

Moscardino, Ughetta, Giovanna Axia, Sara Scrimin, and Fabia Capello. 2007. "Narratives from Caregivers of Children Surviving the Terrorist Attack in Beslan: Issues of Health, Culture, and Resilience." *Social Science & Medicine* 64: 1776–1787.

Motta, Sara C. and Tiina Seppälä. 2016. "Editorial: Feminized Resistances." *Journal of Resistance Studies* 2(2): 5–32.

Murphy, Paul J. 2010. *Allah's Angels: Chechen Women in War*. Naval Institute Press.

Nivat, Anne. 2001. *Chienne de Guerre: A Woman Reporter Behind the Lines of the War in Chechnya*. New York: Public Affairs.

Nussbaum, Martha. 2003. "Compassion & Terror." *Daedalus,* 132(1): 10–26.

Ó Tuathail, Gearóid. 2009. "Placing Blame: Making Sense of Beslan." *Political Geography* 28(1): 4–15.

OECD. 2010. "Situation with asylum-seekers from Russian Federation." OECD Finnish-Russian Civic Forum Working Session 6. Accessed 16 January 2017. http://www.osce.org/home/71764?download=true.

Parashar, Swati. 2011. "Embodied 'Otherness' and Negotiations of Difference." In "The Forum: Emotion and the Feminist IR Researcher," edited by C. Sylvester. *International Studies Review* 13(4): 696–99.

Parashar, Swati. 2015. "Anger, War and Feminist Storytelling." In *Emotions, Politics and War*, edited by Linda Åhäll and Thomas Gregory, 71–85. New York: Routledge.

Penttinen, Elina. 2013. *Joy and International Relations: A New Methodology*. London and New York: Routledge.

Petersen, Roger. 2011. *Western Intervention in the Balkans: The Strategic Use of Emotion in Conflict*. Cambridge: Cambridge University Press.

Pinkola Estés, Clarissa. 1992. *Women Who Run with the Wolves: Myths and Stories of the Wild Woman Archetype*. Ballantine Books.

Politkovskaya, Anna. 2003. *A Small Corner of Hell: Dispatches from Chechnya*. Chicago and London: The University of Chicago Press.

Puumala, Eeva, Tarja Väyrynen, Antitta Kynsilehto and Samu Pehkonen. 2011. "Events of the Body Politic: A Nancian Reading of Asylum-seekers' Bodily Choreographies and Resistance." *Body & Society* 17(4), 83–104.

Ramachandran, V.S and Sandra Blakeslee. 1998. *Phantoms in the Brain: Probing the Mysteries of the Human Mind*. New York: William Morrow and Company, Inc.

Rancière, Jacques. 2009. *The Emancipated Spectator*. London and New York: Verso.

Rancière, Jacques. 2008. Vapautunut katsoja (Finnish translation of *Le Spectateur Emapncipé*). Helsinki: Tutkijaliitto [2016].

Raubisko, Ieva. 2009. "Religious Ideology and Islamic Practices in Chechnya." *Journal of the Anthropological Society of Oxford Online* 1(1): 71–93.

Regamey, Amandine. 2014. "Rereading Human Rights Reports: Material Violence in Chechnya 1999-2001." In *Chechnya at War and Beyond,* edited by Anne Le Huérou, Aude Merlin, Amandine Regamey, Elisabeth Sieca-Kozlowski, 200–219. Oxon and New York: Routledge.

Rizzolatti, Giacomo and Laila Craighero. 2004. "The Mirror Neuron System." *Annual Review of Neuroscience* 27: 196–92

Rothman, Jay. 1997. *Resolving Identity-Based Conflict in Nations, Organizations, and Communities*. San Francisco: Jossey-Bass Publishers.

Rouhiainen, Leena. 2008. "Somatic dance as a means of cultivating ethically embodied subjects." *Research in Dance Education* 9(3): 241–56.

Rousseva, Valentina. 2004. "Rape and Sexual Assault in Chechnya." *Culture, Society, Praxis* 3(1): 64–67.

Russell, John. 2007. *Chechnya - Russia's 'War on Terror'*. Oxon: Routledge.

Saarela, Miiamaaria, Yevhen Hlushchuk, Amanda Williams, Martin Schürmann, Eija Kalso, and Riitta Hari. 2007. "The Compassionate Brain: Humans Detect Intensity of Pain from Another's Face." *Cerebral Cortex* 17(1): 230–37.

Sacks, Oliver. 2000. *Seeing Voices: A Journey into the World of the Deaf*. New York: Vintage Books.

Sacks, Oliver. 2008. *Musicophilia: Tales of Music and the Brain, Revised and Expanded Edition.* Vintage Books.

Saeidi, Shirin and Heather M. Turcotte. 2011. "Politicizing Emotions: Historicizing Affective Exchange and Feminist Gatherings." In *The Forum: Emotion and the Feminist IR Researcher*, edited by Christine Sylvester. *International Studies Review* 13(4): 693–95.

Salmon, Karen and Richard A. Bryant. 2002. "Posttraumatic Stress Disorder in Children: The Influence of Developmental Factors." *Clinical Psychology Review* 22(2): 163–188.

Salter, Mark B. and Can E. Mutlu. 2013. *Research Methods in Critical Security Studies.* London and New York: Palgrave.

Scrimin, Sara, Giovanna Axia, Fabia Capello, Ughetta Moscardino, Alan M. Steinberg, Robert S. Pynoos. 2006. "Posttraumatic reactions among injured children and their caregivers 3 months after the terrorist attack in Beslan." *Psychiatry Research* 141(3): 333–36.

Seierstad, Åsne. 2007. *The Angel of Grozny: Orphans of a Forgotten War.* Translated by Nadia Christensen. New York: Basic Books.

Shapiro, Michael J. 2009. *Cinematic Geopolitics*. London and New York: Routledge.

Shepherd, Laura. 2013. *Gender, Violence and Popular Culture: Telling Stories*. Oxon and New York: Routledge.

Sheets-Johnstone, Maxine. 2011. *The Primacy of Movement*. Amsterdam: John Benjamins Publishing Company.

Slote, Michael. 2007. *Ethics of Care and Empathy.* Oxon and New York: Routledge.

Speckhard, Anne and Khapta Akhmedova. 2006a. "Black Widows: The Chechen Female Suicide Terrorists." In *Female Suicide Bombers: Dying for Equality?,* edited by Yoram Schweitzer, 63–80. Jaffee Center for Strategic Studies (JCSS), Tel Aviv University.

Speckhard, Anne and Khapta Akhmedova. 2006b. "The Making of a Martyr: Chechen Suicide Terrorism." *Journal of Studies in Conflict & Terrorism*, 29(5) 429–92.

Sylvester, Christine. 2011. "Experiencing War: an Introduction." In *Experiencing War,* edited by Christine Sylvester, 1–7. New York and Oxon: Routledge.

Sylvester, Christine. 2013a. "Experiencing War: A Challenge for International Relations." *Cambridge Review of International Affairs* 26(4): 669–74.

Sylvester, Christine. 2013b. *War as Experience*. New York and Oxon: Routledge

Sylvester, Christine. 2015. "Avoiding the 'Killing' of Lives: Representations in Academia and Fiction." Interview in *Studying the Agency of Being Governed*, edited by Stina Hansson, Sofie Hellberg and Maria Stern, 64–74. Oxon and New York: Routledge.

Szczepanikova, Alice. 2014. "Chechen Refugees in Europe: How Three Generations of Women Settle in Exile." In *Chechnya at War and Beyond* edited by Anne Le Huérou, Aude Merlin, Amandine Regamey, and Elisabeth Sieca-Kozlowski, 256–73. Oxon and New York: Routledge.

Seppälä, Tiina. 2016. Feminizing Resistance, Decolonizing Solidarity: Contesting Neoliberal Development in the Global South. *Journal of Resistance Studies* 2(1): 12–47.

Seppälä, Tiina. 2017. "On 'Outsourcing' the Political in Political Science." *Social Identities* 23(6): 1–16.

Smith, Andrea. 2013. "The Problem with Privilege." *Andrea Smith's Blog*, 14 August. Accessed 1 May 2017. https://andrea366.wordpress.com/2013/08/14/the-problem-with-privilege-by-andrea-smith/

Stoppard, Tom. 1982. *The Real Thing*. Audible. Audiobook.

Tarr, Bronwyn , Jacques Launay, Emma Cohen and Robin Dunbar. 2015. "Synchrony and Exertion during Dance Independently Raise Pain Threshold and Encourage Social Bonding." *Biology Letters* 11(10).

Tchernookova, Alice. 2015. "This Journalist Spoke to Chechens Living in the Shadow of the War." *Vice Magazine,* 24 June. Accessed 1 May 2017. https://www.vice.com/en_au/article/twenty-years-after-a-devastating-war-what-has-become-of-chechnya

Terloeva, Milana. 2006. *Danser sur les Ruines: Une Jeunesse Tchétchène.* Hachette Litératures. Kindle ed.

The Lotus Sutra (n.d.). Translated by Watson Burton. New York: Columbia University Press [1993].

Thompson, Evan. 2007. *Mind in Life: Biology, Phenomenology and the Sciences of Mind.* Cambridge: The Belknap Press of Harvard University Press.

Tishkov, Valery. 2004. *Chechnya: Life in a War Torn Society.* Berkeley: University of California Press.

Tribeca Film Festival. 2005. "Film Guide: COCA-The Dove from Chechnya." *Tribeca Film Festival.* Accessed 15 January 2017 https://tribecafilm.com/filmguide/archive/512cdc2d1c7d76e04600029a-coca-the-dove-from-chechn

Ure, Michael and Mervyn Frost. 2014. *Politics of Compassion.* Oxon: Routledge.

Valdesolo, Percarlo and DeSteno. 2011. "Synchrony and the Social Tuning of Compassion." *Emotion* 11(2): 262-266.

Van der Kolk, Bessel. 2014. *The Body Keeps the Score: Brain, Mind and Body in the Healing of Trauma.* Audible. Audiobook.

Van der Vet, Freek. 2013. "Transitional Justice in Chechnya: NGO Political Advocacy for Implementing Chechen Judgments of the European Court of Human Rights." *Review of Central and East European Law* 38(3-4): 363–388

Van Munster, Rens and Casper Sylvest. 2013. "Documenting International Relations: Documentary Film and the Creative Arrangement of Perceptibility." *International Studies Perspectives* 16(3): 229–45.

Varela, Francisco J., Evan Thompson and Eleanor Rosch. 1993. *The Embodied Mind: Cognitive Science and Human Experience.* Cambridge and Massachusetts: The MIT Press.

Vastapuu, Leena. 2017. *Hope Is Not Gone Altogether: The Roles and Reintegration of Young Female War Veterans in Liberia.* Turku: University of Turku. Doctoral dissertation.

Von Dietze, Erich and Angelica Orb. 2000. "Compassionate Care: A Moral Dimension of Nursing." *Nursing Inquiry* 7(3): 166–74.

Von Scheve, Christian and Mikko Salmela. 2014. *Collective Emotions: Perspectives from Psychology, Philosophy and Sociology.* Oxford University Press.

Väyrynen, Tarja. 2013. "Corporeal Migration." In *Research Methods in Critical Security Studies,* edited by Mark B. Salter and Can E. Mutlu, 169–72. London and New York: Palgrave.

Väyrynen, Tarja, Samu Pehkonen, Anitta Kynsilehto, Eeva Puumala and Tiina Vaittinen. 2016. *Choreographies of Resistance: Mobilities, Bodies, Politics.* London: Rowman and Littlefield.

Walker, Shaun. 2017. "Chechen police 'have rounded up more than 100 suspected gay men.'" *Guardian,* 2 April. Accessed 11 April 2017.https://www. theguardian.com/world/2017/apr/02/chechen-police-rounded-up-100-gay-men-report-russian-newspaper-chechnya?CMP=share_btn_tw

Weldes, Jutta and Christina Rowley. 2015. "So, How Does Popular Culture Relate to World Politics?." In *Popular Culture and World Politics: Theories, Methods, Pedagogies*, edited by Federica Caso and Caitlin Hamilton, 11–34. Bristol: E-International Relations.

Welland, Julia. 2015. "Compassionate Soldiering and Comfort." In *Emotions, Politics and War*, edited by Linda Åhäll and Thomas Gregory, 115–127. New York: Routledge.

Wibben, Annick T. R. 2011. *Feminist Security Studies: A Narrative Approach.* London: Routledge.

Yun, Kyongsik, Katsumi Watanabe and Shinsuke Shimojo. 2012. "Interpersonal Body and Neural Synchronization as a Marker of Implicit Social Interaction." *Scientific Reports* 2.

Zalewski, Marysia. 2015. "Stories of Pain and Longing: Reflecting on Emotion, Boundaries and Feminism through Carrie Mathison and Carrie White." In *Emotions, Politics and War*, edited by Linda Åhäll and Thomas Gregory, 32–42. New York: Routledge.

Films

Barzakh. 2011. Directed by Mantas Kvedaravicius.

Children of Beslan. 2005. Directed by Ewa Ewart and Leslie Woodhead.

Coca – The Dove from Chechnya: Europe in a Denial of War. 2005. Directed by Eric Bergraut.

The 3 Rooms of Melancholia. 2004. Directed by Pirjo Honkasalo (Original title: *Melancholian 3 huonetta*).

12. 2007. Directed by Nikita Mikhalkov.

Note on Indexing

E-IR's publications do not feature indexes. If you are reading this book in paperback and want to find a particular word or phrase you can do so by downloading a free PDF version of this book from the E-IR website.

View the e-book in any standard PDF reader such as Adobe Acrobat Reader (pc) or Preview (mac) and enter your search terms in the search box. You can then navigate through the search results and find what you are looking for. In practice, this method can prove much more effective than consulting an index.

If you are using apps (or a device) to read our e-books, you should also find word search functionality in those.

You can find all of our e-books at: http://www.e-ir.info/publications

www.ingramcontent.com/pod-product-compliance
Lightning Source LLC
Chambersburg PA
CBHW050724030426

42336CB00012B/1413